Caffettiera

Zuviera

Piatto

Tondino

Scaldavivande

Silver

THE SMITHSONIAN ILLUSTRATED LIBRARY OF ANTIQUES

General Editor: Brenda Gilchrist

Silver

Jessie McNab

COOPER-HEWITT MUSEUM

The Smithsonian Institution's National Museum of Design

ENDPAPERS
Design for set of tableware by Pietro Belli. Pencil, pen and black ink, and gray watercolor. Italian, Rome, 1815-30. Cooper-Hewitt Museum, purchase, Friends of the Museum Fund

FRONTISPIECE
The magnolia vase designed by John T. Curran was a Tiffany & Company entry at the 1893 World's Columbian Exposition in Chicago. The opulence of color and materials, choice of decorative motifs and especially the "Toltec" handles strike a Central American theme. The top-heavy form is characteristic of the 1890s. Embellished with opals and enameled work. American, 1893. Height: 78.7 cm. (31 in.). Metropolitan Museum of Art, New York, gift of Mrs. Winthrop Atwell, 1899

For Elizabeth

Art Direction, Design: JOSEPH B. DEL VALLE

Text Editor: NANCY AKRE

Contents

1   Introduction

For five thousand years silver has been recognized as a very special substance. Since Roman times silver substitutes have been produced, starting with pewter and silver-plated bronze, and including numerous more modern substances such as nickel, chrome, silver-plated base metals and stainless steel. Even platinum at first was seen as just another silver-colored metal. Yet silver has never been supplanted in its special appeal.

Throughout its history, silver has had a rather narrow range of uses, being reserved primarily for objects designed to inspire a sense of respect—even awe—in religious, military, domestic or purely personal contexts. Archaeologists and historians politely differ over whether silver was first pursued for its undeniable beauty or whether it merely happened to be one of the metals discovered in the great surge of technological advance that took place in the ancient Near East in the fourth millennium B.C. and, being essentially useless for weapons or any stress-bearing function, was relegated to that of ornament.

There are also two schools of thought concerning the origins of metallurgy itself, of which silver production was a part. Diffusionists believe that technical improvements spread from a prime place of innovation, whereas a second school of thought holds that inventions occurred independently in separate places among peoples who cannot be proved to have had contact with one another. It is this writer's view that silver's *color*, a color like no other, was considered essential to the life-supporting aspects of religious ritual among early agricultural civilizations and that this notion was behind the activities that culminated in the discovery of silver.

Silver antiques are among the most valuable and versatile of collectibles. Old, beautiful and rare objects that can still be used in domestic surroundings, these silver wares are relics of four hundred

Colorplate 1.
The decorative effect of this Queen Anne-style kettle, with its accompanying salver, spirit lamp and tripod stand, the last two cast in solid silver, comes largely from the metal itself. Made in London by Simon Pantin. English, 1724–5. Height of tripod: 64.1 cm. (25¼ in.). Height of kettle and spirit lamp: 39.4 cm. (15½ in.). Metropolitan Museum of Art, New York, gift of Irwin Untermyer, 1968

years of the cultural past of Europe and colonial and post-colonial America. Such objects are discussed in greater detail than those surviving from earlier periods. The story of silver would be incomplete, however, without a brief glance at its use in the long procession of early cultures from which the West inherited the art of working the metal. European and English silver wares from Roman times to the beginning of the seventeenth century are considered antiquities rather than antiques, and are to be found almost exclusively in museums, cathedrals, church treasuries and state collections of regalia or among the prized property of such long-lived foundations as universities and colleges. Very few silver antiquities are held in private collections.

We should not forget that during the course of its history, silver has also been employed in a great many ways other than for making those objects we now call antiques and antiquities. It has been used as silver leaf for application to furniture and to plate glass (in the production of mirrors); as silver and silver-gilt threads for tapestries, silks, laces, embroideries and silk carpets; as inlay on steel armor; as silver foil under the polychrome of baroque wooden statues; and as a most beautiful and ethereal draftsman's tool for silver-point drawings. As early as the sixteenth century, silver was also consumed in the production of lustres for some majolicas.

A vast literature, ranging from general to very specialized works, exists for the guidance of those interested in silver antiques. The Reading and Reference section at the end of this book categorizes the types of available literature and gives a few titles in each section as a starting point for further reading.

Figure 1.
A workshop specializing in domestic silver wares. Engraving by Étienne Delaune, Augsburg, 1576. Bibliothèque Nationale, Paris.

Three journeymen, an apprentice and the master are shown engaged in typical activities. All are fashionably dressed and three of the adults wear poniards at their belts, a symbol of their high social status. Theirs is, nevertheless, a manual occupation. The apprentice and one silversmith are using bellows to intensify the heat in the forge. Behind them, ranged on the left wall, are files, snips and a variety of hammers. At their feet are tongs, a pile of silver bars and a mold for ingots. In the foreground a silversmith is planishing a beaker, holding the side over a stake set into a section of tree trunk. Other stakes, variously shaped for particular purposes, can be seen on each side of the doorway and above the hammers on the left wall. The pointed shafts of the stakes fit into the holes in the wood block and are thus held secure and can be easily changed. Between the doorway and the window, on the floor, is a stake with a rounded end for working on rounded forms. In the right corner is a drawbench; a plate pierced with successively smaller holes through which metal was drawn to make wire hangs on the wall above. Two mallets of wood, or of rawhide (used for work requiring the gentlest of hammer taps), hang above the feather fan over the drawbench.

At the work table a worker is chasing a design on a large dish. A sandbag cushions the dish. His wrist is flexible, and he holds the chasing hammer with a light grasp, poised above the punch, so different from the grip and motion of the worker in the foreground. Near to hand on the table are a canister of rodlike punches used in chasing, a hare's foot for dusting (another hangs from the table) and three gravers. At the window the master converses with a potential patron. In accordance with Augsburg regulations, which were similar to those all over Europe, the interior of the workshop and the forge had to be visible from the street. On a shelf above the window are some finished wares.

Figure 2.
A workshop specializing in small gold objects, jewelry, chains and rings. Engraving by Étienne Delaune, Augsburg, 1576. Bibliothèque Nationale, Paris.

The journeyman at the right is enameling an object at the forge—the piece is inside a protective box, which he holds in the heat with tongs. To the left, the drawbench is in action, with the pierced plate set behind two braces. All three workers at the table wear leather aprons to catch the particles of gold dust or filings that fall.

2   The Working of Silver

In a sense, a consolidated mass of silver is an artificial product, distilled by much labor from its natural surroundings. Silver is rarely found in its native state in nuggets or chunks, as gold can be, but occurs as shining foils and filaments in rocky matrixes or dispersed and invisible in various compounds. The sources of silver are distributed widely over the globe, but it was those that gave visual promise of their content—the silver-bearing ores and dusts—that were naturally the first to be worked. Galena, a lead sulphide in the form of a sparkling rock that could be easily collected from surface deposits, was the foundation of the silver-producing industry of the Near East as early as the fourth millennium B.C. (colorplate 2). In antiquity the lead mines in Asia Minor, Persia, Greece, Spain and central Europe were important suppliers of silver, particularly the mines at Laurion, in Attica, which were worked during the fifth century B.C. In the tenth century A.D. the mines of central Europe were reactivated, and those of Austria and Hungary became especially productive during the sixteenth century.

As the supply of galena in one mine neared exhaustion, the search would begin for other sources. The news that silver had been discovered in the New World was met with excitement throughout Europe in the sixteenth century, although it took considerable effort for the precious metal to be mined and transported across the Atlantic. Silver in North and South America is found in rock embedments, often far below the earth's surface. Until the last century, pickaxes and hammers had to be used to break up the rocky matrix that contained the veins of metal—work that was slow, back-breaking and often dangerous, with the threat of cave-ins and flooding.

Once the ore had been hewn from the surrounding rock, it was broken into chunks that could be hauled to the smeltery. There it

Colorplate 2.
Galena, the ore in its natural state. Found in all parts of the world, galena is the prime material for the production of silver. The galena deposits of Asia Minor were especially extensive and were the first to be exploited more than five thousand years ago. The history of silver production begins with the discovery that the shining particles in galena contained lead, within which existed, in an intimate bond, a white, more shining and noble metal—silver. American Museum of Natural History, New York

was crushed, pulverized and, finally, washed and sieved in preparation for roasting, which disengages the silver-bearing lead from the ore. To remove silver from galena, a triple heating process is necessary. The first heating melts out the metallic content from the rocky dust; the second separates the lead-silver content from other metallic substances in the crude lead; the third extracts silver from the lead. This process has been in use since antiquity. The treatment of copper ores and the extraction of silver from the natural gold-silver alloy electrum have also been a part of silver production since ancient times. More recently the extraction of silver from a number of hitherto unsuspected hosts, such as silver sulphides, has been achieved by chemical and electrolytic methods.

Besides the characteristics that we find so beautiful in silver—its brilliance, its reflective powers and its purity of color—the metal has three properties that facilitate its being worked into objects. It is meltable, allowing it to flow while molten into a shape that it will retain when cooled, and it is both malleable and ductile. Next to gold, silver is the most malleable and most ductile of all the metals. A gram of pure silver can be beaten into a sheet of foil 0.00025 millimeters thick or drawn into a wire over one mile long. Although obviously vulnerable to damage, silver objects are capable of withstanding years, even centuries, of use and exposure.

Pure silver is too soft to be of use in making coinage, jewelry or objects that must withstand daily wear. To remedy this, the metal is mixed in an alloy. Copper has proved to be a good strengthener for the silversmith's purposes; added to silver in the proper proportion, it hardens the silver without rendering it too brittle or adulterating the "pure" white color that is one of the metal's most desirable features. An alloy of silver and copper will retain its characteristic color until the amount of copper exceeds 45 percent, although the metal becomes less malleable and oxidizes more rapidly as the amount of copper increases. The proportion of silver in the alloy is stated in terms of the silver's "fineness." Sterling silver is 925 parts fine, or 925 parts silver to 75 parts copper. In colonial America, where silver was obtained mostly from melted coins, the purity of the alloyed metal varied.

Although the styles of their wares varied, the tools and techniques used by silversmiths in the Near East in 3500 B.C. were not too different from those used by silversmiths up to industrialization in the eighteenth century. An understanding of the processes involved in converting a bar of silver into a beautiful and functional object, only some of which are discernible in the finished piece, enhances one's appreciation of the silversmith's accomplishments. When we look at a teapot or an inkstand, a caudle cup or a candelabrum, and visualize all the challenges met by the silversmith as he fashioned these articles, the excellence of the work can be determined.

Figure 3.
A silver workshop of the mid-eighteenth century as shown in Diderot's *Encyclopédie ou Dictionnaire raisonné des sciences, des arts et des métiers*. This illustration is from volume 8, published in Paris in 1765. The Metropolitan Museum of Art, Thomas J. Watson Library.

The essential activities are unchanged from a sixteenth-century workshop, as in figure 1. Shown here are workers: (a) pouring molten silver into an ingot mold; (e) battering a disc from an ingot; (b) raising a beaker supported over a suitable stake, or anvil (the worker is seated in the goldsmith's habitual posture, with his foot stuck out and resting on its edge); (c) planishing a dish. In (d) the stake has not been included so the worker appears to be working without support, in mid-air. In the background is the forge with massive bellows attached.

We do not have a complete set of tools from the earliest days of silverworking, but the hematite hammers and anvils excavated from the Royal Cemetery at Ur indicate that the tools used in the third millennium B.C. were no less hard than eighteenth-century steel tools. Weights, scales, punches, dies, pliers, hammers, blowpipes, tongs and grinding stones have been needed from the earliest times. In 1722 when the American silversmith John Coney died, the inventory of tools and stock in trade in his Boston shop included two touchstones for testing the fineness of silver and one for testing that of gold, bellows for increasing the temperature of the fire in the forge, tongs for handling hot objects, crucibles for melting metal, skillets and molds for casting, compasses, shears, and various anvils, stakes, files, pliers, vises, saws, drills, molds, punches, drawing irons, chisels, stamps and gravers. The

inventory also listed 112 hammers for "Raising, Pibling, Swolling, Hollowing, Creasing [and] Planishing."

The silversmith began his labors by alloying bars of fine (pure) silver at the forge. When the silver-copper mixture reached a white-hot, molten state, it was poured into molds of standard sizes, producing ingots, or bars, of silver. Sheet silver, which is the basis of all hollow wares, was obtained by reducing ingots to a sheet of even thickness by a process of battering with large hammers. As the silversmith hammered, the crystalline structure of the silver was altered, creating internal stress and causing the metal to become brittle. To restore its malleability, the silver was then *annealed*—that is, heated to a cherry red color—which freed the atoms to rearrange themselves once again in their natural order. Annealing was a critical step, for if the metal was not reheated often enough or to a high enough temperature, it would crack under the stress of the hammer; on the other hand, if the metal was left at the fire too long, it could begin to melt. When the silver turned cherry red, it was removed from the fire with tongs and plunged into a cooling bath. Finally, after the metal had been forged into a sheet of even thickness, the silversmith used shears to cut out a disc of silver.

There were two common methods by which a seamless hollow vessel could be formed from a disc of sheet silver—*sinking* and *raising*. Sinking, the simpler method of the two, was used to produce shallow wares such as bowls. To sink a bowl, a disc of silver was hammered into the hollowed-out depression of a large, stable block of wood or a tree trunk. The silversmith began hammering on the outside edge of the disc and worked around and around, toward the center of the bowl. The silver at the center received less hammering and was usually thicker than that forming the sides of the vessel, a feature that was adapted to advantage in the design of the round-bottomed traveling cups of the seventeenth and early eighteenth centuries, where the extra thickness at the bottom of the cup acted as a stabilizer.

A deeper vessel, such as a coffeepot or beaker, had to be raised on a stake. Before raising began, the disc of silver received preliminary shaping on a stake grooved for crimping metal. To crimp the metal, the disc was held against the grooved stake, then hammered into the groove with a beaked hammer, the crimps being spaced at intervals to create a fluted vessel. Next, the silversmith tilted the inside of this fluted form against the raising stake and proceeded to hammer the exterior surface onto the stake with row after row of taps, working alternately in a clockwise and counterclockwise direction to prevent distortion. Gradually the hammering smoothed out the fluting and pushed the metal upward to form the sides of the vessel. A good silversmith could raise the body of a coffeepot in a morning, interrupting his hammering dozens of times to anneal the vessel in the fire.

The next process, after raising or sinking, was *planishing*. This removed the marks left by the raising hammer. The planishing hammer had a slightly convex, broad head that effectively smoothed out surface irregularities.

Another, quicker method for making simple hollow forms was to *seam* the metal. To make a beaker, for instance, a rectangular sheet of silver was curved into a cylinder and the seam soldered vertically. Then the base was soldered in, using little chips of silver with a higher alloy content and lower melting point than the metal of the vessel itself. In order to melt the solder chips, the beaker had to be heated to a glowing cherry red. At the crucial moment, after the solder had melted and flowed into the air space of the joint but before the vessel had overheated, the silversmith removed the object from the fire with his tongs and immersed it in a quenching bath.

In the second half of the eighteenth century rolling mills were invented that could produce silver sheet of fairly thin gauge, which proved an economy in metal as well as in labor. Although silver sheet was at first employed only for making straight-sided shapes, it was soon being used to make pieces that were shaped and decorated in one operation, since the metal was thin enough to be forced into a die.

Once the silversmith had given the object its basic form, he began the work necessary to ornament it. Decorative effects on silver can be divided into those that exploit its color and those that are achieved by manipulating or modifying the surface of the metal. The most fundamental of all decorative techniques is *polishing*. The planishing hammer can give a good surface to an object, but perfect luminosity can be gained only with polish. Originally, polishing was done entirely with abrasives and smoothing stones of greater and greater degrees of softness. In European, English and American silver, however, the surface was first filed all over to remove minute irregularities and to smooth the edges of the tiny facets left by the planishing hammer; next, it was rubbed with a coarse abrasive such as pumice, and then with a smooth stone such as Ayr stone; finally, it was buffed. French silver was given a beautiful polish by *burnishing*, or compacting the surface by pressing it with the rounded edge of a steel blade. Because French silver was very pure, having only 5 percent alloy, it was rather soft. Burnishing gave the surface a greater density and helped offset its liability to superficial scratching and wear.

Sometimes, particularly on old spoons and objects made before the middle of the eighteenth century, the marks of the planishing hammer can still be seen in a honeycomb pattern; this indicates that the piece was either not polished at all or only slightly so. Tarnish may reveal such a pattern, and although these marks impair the beauty of highly finished and elegant works, they do not disfigure simple pieces. When the honeycombing is very regular and obvious it is an example of a

Figure 4.
Marks of the planishing hammer (detail of plate 42)

decorative effect called *martelé* (hammered), which was used during the late nineteenth and early twentieth centuries by craftsmen who were ideologically committed to a return to handwork. Although meant to emphasize the fact that a piece was handmade, the effect was soon imitated on factory-made wares.

An early and very beautiful use of color in silver design was achieved by combining silver with gold, contrasting the white silvery light with the yellow golden one. In very ancient times the effect was achieved by combining areas of silver with areas of gold, but by Roman times it was already being gained by gilding the silver in the required areas, a technique usually called by its old name, parcel-gilt, meaning simply partly gilt. With time and wear, the gold pales to a quiet lemon color or disappears almost completely, and the silver becomes dull, with minute surface scratches (see colorplate 8), so that contrasts in old parcel-gilt objects often are not as arresting as they must once have been (see colorplate 23 for an example of recent parcel-gilding). This is a disadvantage, of course, and one not shared by pieces made entirely of silver, where the surface polish dulls evenly over the whole piece with no loss of visual effect.

Of the several methods used to gild silver, the most common was mercury gilding, by which an amalgam of gold and mercury was applied as a paste to the surface to be gilded and the mercury then vaporized by heat. In an earlier method a linen rag soaked in a chloride of gold was dried and burned, then the ashes were rubbed into the surface of the silver. Unfortunately, far too many silver-gilt objects that have become worn have been re-gilt—a practice that can usually be detected by the inappropriate brightness and fullness of the gold, the absence of wear on handles and rims where one would expect to find at least some (even on pieces that may have had an extraordinarily sheltered existence) and a redder tint to the gold. Old gilding, even when fresh, had a yellower color than was popular in the nineteenth century, when re-gilding became common with the use of electroplating.

Enameling, a decorative technique always popular for jewelry, was revived by silversmiths in the nineteenth century, first for ecclesiastical pieces and then, in the second half of the century, for secular objects, too. To incorporate enamelwork into silver, the most secure method is *champlevé*, in which areas of metal are excavated to form a decorative pattern, then filled with colored vitreous pastes that are fired and polished. Painted enamels, which can give more delicate effects, are extremely vulnerable (see colorplate 21).

A dramatic effect, both on silver and on silver gilt, can be produced with *niello*, a powdered alloy of silver, copper, lead and sulphur that is rubbed into a design incised on the vessel's surface and then fused with the silver by heat. Usually the design appears as black on a silver or gilt

Figure 5.
Martelé (detail of plate 89)

Figure 6.
Champlevé (detail of plate 14)

Figure 7.
Niello (detail of plate 7)

background, but sometimes the background has been nielloed, leaving the pattern in shining metal. An ancient technique, niello was reintroduced during the Arab occupation of the Iberian peninsula. It became particularly popular during the fifteenth century in Italy and during the sixteenth in Germany, where its Arabic heritage continued to be felt in the style of the designs chosen by silversmiths. Nielloing was also long favored in Russia; in the nineteenth century it was used there with great success to execute topographical scenes and cityscapes, often on silver-gilt backgrounds.

A newer method of coloring silver, *oxydization*, was introduced in the middle of the nineteenth century in France and Germany and quickly became popular in England and Russia as well. Oxydization imparts a dull, grayish surface coloration to the silver; it is primarily employed to set off areas of highly polished silver. The effect is achieved by the application of a chemical solution that creates a layer of silver sulphide on the surface of the silver. The depth of the color achieved is determined by the strength of the solution used and the length of time that the solution is left on the metal.

In addition to introducing color, silversmiths use a variety of techniques for decorating the surface of the silver itself, either by cutting metal from, applying it to, or manipulating the surface of the object. One of the earliest and simplest techniques for decorating silver is *engraving*: extracting thin filaments of silver with a sharp tool (a scorper or graver) to form a decorative pattern on the surface of the metal. The graver is a diamond-shaped steel rod, set in a wooden handle; the rod's end is cut off diagonally, giving a sharp point to the cutting edge. Until the mid-sixteenth century engraving on European and English silver was somewhat crude, but by the late sixteenth century it had become highly refined and was used to carry out entire pictorial compositions. Engraving was also favored for heraldic work. Following a universal code, fine lines and dots were used to represent the colors in a coat of arms. Today, engraving is used chiefly for inscriptions.

In another form of decoration, known as *pricking*, a point is driven into the silver over and over again to build up a design. Pricking was used as an accompanying decoration of great delicacy on highly ornamented pieces, and also for dates and initials and in certain areas of pictorial work. Although the results were often charming, pricking has not been much employed since the seventeenth century.

In *flat chasing*—one of a group of associated techniques using punches to create a surface design—the metal is indented in a linear pattern rather than cut away, as it is in engraving. An early example of chasing is seen on the Elam bull (see colorplate 3). Chasing punches are steel rods that come to a small face, perhaps no more than one-sixteenth to one-eighth of an inch wide and only half again as high.

Figure 8.
Engraving (detail of plate 13)

Figure 9.
Pricking (detail of plate 22)

Figure 10.
Flat chasing (detail of plate 12)

A chasing hammer (which is lighter and has more spring than either a planishing or a raising hammer) is used to tap the punch along the surface of the metal, leaving a fine, shallow impression from which the design is built up. The stops and starts of the hammer's progress are quite visible on coarse work but more difficult to discern on finer work. Flat chasing, which is not as fine as engraving, is mainly used to outline areas of relief work done with a variety of other punches.

A delightful pattern results from the juxtaposition of highly polished areas of silver with areas that have been intentionally dulled, or broken up into tiny points of light by punches with various patterns engraved on their faces, an effect generally known as *matting*.

In the early seventeenth century quite charming designs were built up by striking the surface of the metal from the back with punches that ended in simple round bosses of different sizes. This produced a raised bead on the top side, and is usually referred to as *embossing*.

Repoussé (meaning pushed out), a method used to create pictorial effects in relief, is the most time-consuming of all of the techniques for surface decoration. The silversmith first flat-chases a design on the surface of the work; this leaves an indented pattern on the upper side and a raised pattern on the underside. He then reverses the piece and, working from the back, punches out the silver within the chased lines to produce a raised effect on the outer side. While the work is in progress, the piece must be supported so that the punches stretch the silver only locally. Usually pitch is applied thickly to the underside of the area to be worked, and the object is further supported on a sandbag. When the first pushing out of the surface has been completed, the pitch is heated and cleaned off, and the worker strengthens the outline of the pattern on the top side by a second application of flat chasing where necessary. Work proceeds this way—from front to back and back to front, using dozens of punches—until the desired effect has been achieved.

Embossing is technically the same as repoussé and is the earlier name for it in the English language. Today there is a tendency to reserve the first term for large, relief designs or for designs that have been stamped into thin silver sheet by a mold or die. This kind of embossing cannot be used on domestic wares, since the thinness of the sheet renders it too fragile unless the object is backed with a packing material such as pitch or plaster. It is effective for such items as brush and mirror backs and filled candlesticks.

Silversmiths used a stamping process in the sixteenth and early seventeenth centuries to make small bands of repeated decoration on strips of thin metal, for application to beakers and cups, the repeats being short and quite apparent. The designs were simple geometric ones (see colorplate 9) or more pictorial ones, and they all reveal a

Figure 11.
Matting (detail of plate 21)

Figure 12.
Repoussé (detail of plate 16)

Figure 13.
Stamping (detail of plate 45)

Figure 14.
Casting (detail of plate 47)

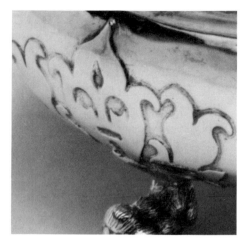

Figure 15.
Cut-card work (detail of plate 26)

charming inventiveness. Since the necessary dies were of steel, they were probably made by toolmakers rather than silversmiths and supplied to the trade, for the same designs can be seen on the work of different silversmiths.

High relief decoration can also be achieved by *casting*, although this requires more metal than the repoussé ornamentation. Small cast parts, such as finials, spouts, feet, handles and openwork bands, were long in use, as were silver sculptures. In the seventeenth century, casting was used for silver furnishings such as chandeliers, and in the eighteenth century, during the rococo period, cast relief additions were soldered onto raised or cast bodies of highly decorated wares. Although their names are unknown and unsung, the artists who carved the wooden models from which molds were made for casting the metal were indirectly responsible for the élan of the finished work. They were probably independent artisans not employed in the silversmith's shop itself, although many may have worked regularly to the orders of a particular silversmith.

Cut-card work—a raised effect resembling low relief but more sparing of silver than casting and requiring less work than repoussé on a hollow form—was developed in France in the seventeenth century and remained a popular ornamentation into the eighteenth century. With this procedure, a relief shape was first made in repoussé on a flat sheet, then cut free and soldered onto the piece. Flatter cut-card work, often with a complicated outline, was an early adaptation of this technique that became especially favored in England.

Acid etching, first used in Germany and Hungary in the sixteenth century, was originally intended for decorating armor. The method for etching silver was similar to the process for etching prints: the

Figure 16.
Acid etching (detail of plate 10)

3   Silver in Antiquity

Until a little more than two hundred years ago, evidence for the antiquity of silver rested entirely on written sources such as the Bible and the Homeric epics. The massive tonnage of silver articles that must have been produced in antiquity has largely disappeared, not by decay, for silver does not decay unless it comes into contact with damp earth and the corrosive salts in it, but as a result of being melted down and remodeled into other forms. The only ancient silver that exists today has been recovered accidentally or by archaeological excavation (colorplate 3) from tombs, hoards or settlements that were hastily abandoned before some impending disaster. Our knowledge of silver in antiquity has been gleaned from the fortuitous discovery of these sites, and is consequently incomplete and somewhat speculative. Nevertheless, enough ancient silver has been recovered to show that silverworking reached technical and artistic heights that may have been equaled in later ages but have certainly never been surpassed.

Recent excavations in Bulgaria, Romania and northern Greece have uncovered quantities of pottery with an allover silvery sheen or striking silvery linear decoration. At Sitagroi, in northern Greece, this pottery was dated by the radiocarbon method to about 4650 B.C. In another excavation at Karanovo, Bulgaria, small cones of natural graphite—a lead compound—with very pointed ends were found along with silvery pottery, indicating how the graphite was applied. The pottery showed no sign of use, and the contexts in which it has been found suggest that it was reserved for ritual purposes, along with the gold ritual axes and personal ornaments found in the same tombs. What makes these discoveries so fascinating is the early linkage of gold and silver in sacred uses, and the occurrence, almost a thousand years before the appearance of silver itself, of an appreciation of the color.

Colorplate 3.
Recently discovered objects such as this figure of a kneeling bull give historians an expanded view of the use of silver in the ancient world. The figure was made from fifteen or more pieces of silver sheet, soldered together and modeled from the inside by tooling. The facial lines and design on the skirt are chased. Probably Elamite, c. 3000 B.C. Height: 16.4 cm. (6½ in.). Metropolitan Museum of Art, New York, bequest of Joseph Pulitzer, 1966

4 European and English Silver: The Dark Ages to 1600

The collapse of the Western Roman Empire was gradual, occurring first in the outlying provinces of Britain, Gaul and Spain, and not ending until A.D. 476, when Italy itself became the realm of the barbarian king Odoacer. Judging by the wealth of hoards dating from the long period of barbarian attacks, much domestic silver was hidden or buried in the hope of eventually returning to recover it. The most spectacular hoards to have been found are those from Boscoreale in Italy, from Hildesheim in Prussia, from Mildenhall in England and from Rome on the Esquiline Hill. The last was probably buried at the time of the sack of Rome by Alaric, the Visigoth king, in A.D. 410. As well as a large cosmetic box (plate 4), the cache consisted of an equally imposing embossed casket for jewels, a tall flask, three dishes and a saucepan, a bowl and a knife handle, a buckle and plaques from horse trappings, and four silver-gilt female statues personifying the principal cities of the empire: Rome, Constantinople, Alexandria and Antioch.

When Rome ceased mining, refining and distributing the metal, silver became extremely rare in Europe. Melted coinage probably provided the bullion for the silver doors made for the Vatican Basilica in Rome in about 630, but much of the old Roman silver coinage must have drifted eastward to areas under the firm dominion of the Eastern Empire. Artisans were obliged to migrate eastward, especially to the capital of the Eastern Empire, Constantinople, where extremely beautiful secular and religious plate was wrought during what is called western Europe's Dark Ages (plate 5).

We have little knowledge of silver production in Spain under Islamic occupation and rule during this same early period. Although the currency of the Arab world tended to be gold, the metalwork, with some beautiful exceptions (plate 6), was usually base, and they employed other materials such as glass and fine pottery for eating and toilet utensils.

Colorplate 4.
The scrolling leaf edging, decorative florets and the rigid seated figure on this precious and fragile crozier head are characteristically Gothic; they reflect a style well behind the contemporary Renaissance work that was being done in northern Italian cities. This parcel-gilt piece is embellished with enamelwork. By an anonymous maker in Naples. Italian, 1457. Height: 49.2 cm. (19¼ in.). Metropolitan Museum of Art, New York, gift of J. Pierpont Morgan, 1917

concerned to protect their currencies. They did so by requiring gold-smiths to use both gold and silver in standards of purity no lower than that of each nation's currency.

Secular silver made before the fifteenth century is rare indeed. Silver spoons were turned out in quantity, and wooden bowls with silver rims, known as mazers, were common. Several kinds of ceremonial objects were made: rosewater ewers and basins for hand washing; also large and ornate containers for salt, which was an expensive com-modity in the fifteenth century, and drinking cups. These objects have been preserved primarily in museums and foundations that have had a relatively uninterrupted history, such as the colleges of Oxford and Cambridge and universities elsewhere.

The Italian goldsmiths were extremely active in the fifteenth cen-tury, but few examples of their work in silver exist today. Many of these men became the great architects, painters and sculptors of their day. Certainly in both design and technique the goldsmiths of Florence were far ahead of those outside the Florentine orbit (plate 7), both in Italy (colorplate 4) and beyond the Alps (colorplate 6 and plate 8).

A number of changes occurred in the sixteenth century that were to affect the conditions under which silver was made and also what was made. The quantity of silver being refined rose throughout the cen-tury, first as a result of stepped-up production in the Austrian and German mines controlled by the Fugger family of Augsburg bankers,

7.
Made for the Florentine Convent of the Poor Clares, this processional cross is deco-rated with superb niello plaques that strongly suggest an original design by Antonio Pol-laiuolo, executed by the famous goldsmith Baccio Baldini. Italian, c. 1464–5. Height: 55.2 cm. (21½ in.). Metropolitan Museum of Art, New York, gift of J. Pierpont Morgan, 1917

8.
Wealth based on gold from the West African coast and a firm command of the Eastern spice trade are reflected in the weight and labor expended on this Portu-guese silver-gilt display dish. *Wode wose*, wild men and women of the woods, cavort on the rim of the dish. Made in Lisbon by an unknown maker. Portuguese, c. 1500–1510. Diameter: 26 cm. (10¼ in.). Metropolitan Museum of Art, New York, gift of J. Pier-pont Morgan, 1917

7

8

Colorplate 6.
The sweeping shape and pointed cover of this parcel-gilt beaker reveal Gothic characteristics, as do the enameled flower and scrolling leaf midband and leafy bands of the foot and cover. Made by Hans Greiff in Ingolstadt. German, 1470. Height: 38.5 cm. (15½ in.). Metropolitan Museum of Art, New York, The Cloisters Collection, Purchase, 1950

Colorplate 5.
Gothic chalices differed very little in form from those of the Byzantine period five hundred years earlier. This parcel-gilt ecclesiastical cup creates a solemn and powerful impression, in spite of the mythical monsters disporting around the boss. Signed by Brother Bertinus. Northern European, 1222. Height: 27 cm. (10½ in.). Metropolitan Museum of Art, New York, The Cloisters Collection, Purchase, 1947

9.
Custodias were highly ornate receptacles for the consecrated bread of the Eucharist, reserved for adoration by the faithful. This ornate piece, made in León by Antonio de Arfe, a member of a distinguished family of goldsmiths, shows a combination of late medieval and Italian Renaissance influences. Spanish, 1544. Height: 182.9 cm. (72 in.). Cathedral of Santiago de Compostela

10.
A print by a French master such as Jacques-Androuet Ducerceau (c. 1510–1584) may have inspired the rather open composition of the decoration on this silver-gilt standing beaker. The maker, Eberwein Kossmann of Nuremberg, combined fine matting, acid etching on the foot, repoussé and chased work with cast finials and brackets. German, c. 1580. Height: 54.6 cm. (21½ in.). Metropolitan Museum of Art, New York, gift of J. Pierpont Morgan, 1917

and then, after the middle of the century, with the arrival of vast amounts of silver from the Spanish mines at Potosí in the vice regency of Peru. Although much of the wealth that Spain gained from early discoveries of silver in the New World was owed to the activities of German bankers, the large church *custodias* made in Spain in the sixteenth century show that silver could still be used on a scale never before or since attempted (plate 9). The South American silver that flowed into Germany increased the total volume of precious metal available there, making Nuremberg and Augsburg great silverworking centers by the second half of the century (plate 10). Their goldsmiths provided far more wares than local consumption required, and the surplus was exported to England and all over Europe. The customized market was further reduced when an independent industry arose in Augsburg and Nuremberg that mass-produced and exported printed design sheets for the use of artisans in all mediums, including metalworking. Another important consequence of this abundance of silver was the separation of goldsmiths who chose to work mainly in silver from those who continued to work in gold, with its attendant skills of enameling and setting precious stones; whatever their preferred medium, all goldsmiths received the same training and belonged to the same guilds.

Not only were more goldsmiths working in silver than ever before but many kinds of serviceable new items were produced. This was particularly true in southern Germany, but also in such cities as London and Antwerp. Beakers of all types appeared. Double cups (long a favorite in Germany) were made to stand upon each other, the top one upside down fitting closely over the rim of the lower one; they occur too in the form of hollow animals (plate 11) and birds. The whimsical note was a favorite (colorplate 7), although more serene pieces are also found (plate 12).

The growth of London as a great silverworking city was initiated in the late sixteenth century. The goldsmith's craft was already ancient there, and the guild, which had been under state regulation since the early thirteenth century, was now rich and powerful. London itself was populous, wealthy and a haven for religious refugees. Much of the most up-to-date work was probably done by goldsmiths trained elsewhere (plate 13). Some of London's goldsmiths seem to have specialized in making highly fashionable mounts for exotic pieces such as serpentine bowls, ostrich eggs, nacreous shells, Chinese porcelains and German stoneware tankards. But there was a large production of more ordinary types: spice boxes, wine cups, small standing salts and spoons. The fashion for sea monsters and marine subjects (colorplate 8) in general was derived from Flemish sources, probably from printmakers such as Adriaen Collaert of Antwerp; and it is on English pieces that we see clearly for the first time chased and engraved designs directly inspired by Chinese porcelain (colorplate 9).

10

Colorplate 7.
This silver-gilt ship is a democratized descendant of the great gold and jeweled *nefs* of the Middle Ages—vessels made to hold precious salt and spices that could be used only by the wealthy. Made by Esaias zur Linden, Nuremberg. German, early seventeenth century. Height: 49.5 cm. (19½ in.). Metropolitan Museum of Art, New York, gift of J. Pierpont Morgan, 1917

11

12

13

11.
Leonhard Umbach, an Augsburg goldsmith, displayed whimsy and ingenuity in creating this silver-gilt double cup. The rampant lion can be taken apart at the collar to make one large and one small cup. German, late sixteenth century. Height: 20.3 cm. (8 in.). Metropolitan Museum of Art, New York, gift of J. Pierpont Morgan, 1917

12.
The main decoration of this silver-gilt beaker is done in imitation of the *prunt Pokal* glass-making technique, in which the ornamental tears are made of applied glass. Here they are reserved against a ground of coarse pricking, less fine than the matting that could have been used, but appropriate. The lip of the beaker is chased with a boating scene and engraved with an inscription. By an anonymous maker in Regensburg. German, 1568. Height: 12.7 cm. (5 in.). Toledo Museum of Art, Toledo, Ohio

13.
Silver spice plates as fanciful as this one were intended more for display than for practical purposes. The scene of Abraham and Sarah departing for Egypt was executed by the Flemish engraver Peter Maas while he was living in London. From a set of twelve. English, c. 1560–70 (with Strasbourg marks of a later date added). Diameter: 19.7 cm. (7¾ in.). Metropolitan Museum of Art, New York, gift of C. Ruxton Love, Jr., 1965

Colorplate 8.
A pair of silver-gilt flagons made for Sir
Edward Coke, chief justice of England. An
overall marine theme is carried out in the
decoration, from the scallop shells on the lid
and body of each to the sea monsters at the
foot and lip. By an unknown London maker
whose mark consisted of a branch within a
shield. English, 1597–8. Height: 31.7 cm.
(12 ¼ in.). Metropolitan Museum of Art,
New York, gift of Irwin Untermyer, 1968

Colorplate 9.
This colorful ewer is a converted Chinese
porcelain bottle of the Wan-li period with
the addition of a cast and chased handle,
straps, a molded and stamped footband, a repoussé and chased cover and engraved decoration of Chinese inspiration on the yoke
joining the straps. The ewer was originally
owned by Lord Burghley, secretary to
Queen Elizabeth I. Maker's mark on silver-
gilt mounts, three trefoils voided. English,
c. 1585. Height: 34.6 cm. (13⅝ in.). Metropolitan Museum of Art, New York, Rogers
Fund, 1944

5   The Seventeenth Century: Variations on the Baroque

From the early seventeenth century until a little after the middle of the eighteenth century silver design was influenced by two worlds: that of England and Europe, in which styles were set by the architects and in which furnishings, including silver, were intended to harmonize with the interiors these architects designed (plates 14–16; see also plates 19 and 29); and that of China, which was beset by an almost insatiable demand for porcelain above all, but also for other rarities such as lacquers, silks and jades. The goldsmiths, at one time the only purveyors of luxury wares, now found themselves forced to compete in their designs with these exotic imports. Their solution was to make silver that reproduced Oriental pieces in form and sometimes in decoration too (plates 17, 20, 24, 28 and 30).

Two wars, the Civil War in England (1642–49) and the Thirty Years' War in Germany (1618–48), were the cause of a serious loss of silver plate. Germany was especially slow to recover from the effects of the upheaval and at first attempted little that was new in silver design (plate 18). In England, the Civil War was followed by a brief form of republican government under the victor, Oliver Cromwell, but the monarchy was restored in 1660 with the accession of Charles II. English Restoration silver was noted for its extravagance and showy ornateness. Charles had stayed in both France and Holland during Cromwell's rule. He had witnessed the gaiety and lavishness of the French court and the great sums of money his cousin Louis XIV was able to command, far more than Parliament would think of allowing him. Nevertheless, it was from France that the English court took its styles in dress, deportment and furnishings in the closing decades of the seventeenth century.

From about 1660 to 1689 in France and about 1670 to 1698 in England there was great profligacy in the use of silver. In both countries silversmiths fashioned silver tubs for orangeries; huge salvers;

Colorplate 10.
An example of the great display dishes, or chargers, that were a specialty of Augsburg craftsmen. This silver and silver-gilt dish is adorned with high relief repoussé personifications of the four continents and a central repoussé plaque showing Alexander the Great lamenting the death of King Darius. Made by the renowned master Adolf Gaap in Augsburg. German, 1689. Width: 72.4 cm. (28½ in.). Cooper-Hewitt Museum, gift of the Trustees of the Estate of James Hazen Hyde

29.
Benjamin Pyne—a well-known London
silversmith—may have used designs by a
French refugee architect and *ornemaniste*
who lived in Holland and England, Daniel
Marot, for the arabesque bases of these
andirons. However, he reverts to the baroque
tradition for the upper parts. English, 1697–8.
Height: 54.6 cm. (21½ in.). Metropolitan
Museum of Art, New York, gift of Irwin
Untermyer, 1968

30.
A typically Dutch piece, this silver brandy bowl was made by an unknown silversmith in Haarlem. The grooves describing the side panels were inspired by painted outlines for panel decorations used on Oriental porcelain. Flower designs and figures of embracing babes are defined in ajouré on the cast handles. Dutch, 1682. Width: 21.6 cm. (8½ in.). Metropolitan Museum of Art, New York, Rogers Fund, 1913

equivalent in silver of the flower and fruit paintings in Dutch art—which they admired. Fine engraving—a tradition established in Holland early in the century—remained popular and was well suited to flat surfaces such as book covers, boxes and the sides of tall beakers. Certain shapes were favored by the Dutch and not elsewhere, among them a deep oval bowl with horizontal handles level with the rim, for drinking hot brandy (plate 30).

Repoussé work was greatly admired in Germany as well, but the motifs were often *retardataire*, particularly on provincial silver, with the pomegranate and berry forms retained from the late sixteenth century (plate 31), although more up-to-date flower decoration in the Dutch taste was also used. The revived industry of Augsburg specialized in making large sideboard dishes with heavy repoussé ornamentation (colorplate 10); tankards, rather more elaborate in decoration than the English ones, were also popular (plate 32).

In America, John Hull and Robert Sanderson, the first silversmiths whose work is known to us, joined forces in 1652 as masters of the new Massachusetts mint and as partners in silversmithing. Most of their work was plain, although a caudle cup of about 1660 or later (now in the Museum of Fine Arts in Boston) shows tulips reserved in polished silver against a matted ground in the manner of some contemporary English work, except that the tulips are rather rigid and unnatural. They also made beakers after the Dutch fashion, spoons, small dram cups and at least one tankard.

John Coney (1655–1722) and Jeremiah Dummer (1645–1718) are the first native-born and native-trained silversmiths known in America. They worked in the last quarter of the century, when Boston and its hinterland were prosperous and growing, and the pieces they supplied to the Boston public were not far behind London styling (plate 33). They made a variety of objects, including spoons, standing cups, beakers, caudle cups, tankards, salts, candlesticks, plates, *tazze* (serving

31

31.
Parcel-gilt plate by an unknown Augsburg master, decorated with repoussé fruits and berries arranged around the heads of three Caesars. The condition of the center is typical of damage incurred by domestic use. German, c. 1670–80. Diameter: 29.2 cm. (11½ in.). Metropolitan Museum of Art, New York, gift of Mrs. Lucy W. Drexel, 1889

32.
Repoussé and chased flowers in the Dutch taste adapt to the baroque form of this silver tankard. Made by Hans Lambrecht III, a Hamburg silversmith, the tankard is accented with a forceful S-scroll handle that curves to the skirt of the base. German, c. 1660–70. Height: 21.6 cm. (8½ in.). Metropolitan Museum of Art, New York, Collection Giovanni P. Morosini, presented by his daughter, Giulia, 1932

33.
The corkscrew thumbpiece, the cut-card decoration on the lid and at the base of the handle and the cast and applied cherub's head on the handle tip of this silver tankard by Jeremiah Dummer, the early Boston silversmith, are all features also found on contemporary English work. The D-section handle is hollow. American, c. 1675. Height: 17.8 cm. (7 in.). Metropolitan Museum of Art, New York, anonymous gift, 1954

32

33

34.

35.

34.
Porringers—useful shallow bowls introduced in the seventeenth century—remained in favor in the American colonies into the late eighteenth century. Made by Jacob Hurd in Boston. American, c. 1740. Diameter: 13.5 cm. (5¼ in.). Cooper-Hewitt Museum, gift of Henry Chauncey

35.
The *retardataire* Dutch influence in New York silver can be seen in both the shape and the decoration of this beaker made by Jurian Blanck, Jr. American, c. 1683. Height: 18.6 cm. (7¼ in.). Metropolitan Museum of Art, New York, bequest of A. T. Clearwater, 1933

stands), chocolate pots and sweetmeat boxes. But the most popular and long-lived of all early American silver objects was the porringer (plate 34); it has survived in greater numbers in America than in England, where it originated as a pottery form around the middle of the century.

In 1667, at the end of a maritime war with Holland, England exchanged Surinam, in South America, for the Dutch enclaves of Manhattan Island and Albany. New Amsterdam, renamed New York, soon became very prosperous, partly as a result of trade with the West Indian colonies and Europe. There was an ample supply of silver coinage available—some of it acquired from pirates—and silversmiths fashioned this into heavy, handsome wares. The city only gradually attracted colonists from England, so that the Dutch influence remained strong (plate 35).

During the 1670s and 1680s, Louis XIV's vacillation in his policy toward Protestants caused a continual exodus from France of self-employed craftsmen in the luxury trades. In 1685, after the revocation of the Edict of Nantes, which had guaranteed the political rights of French Protestants since 1598, this trickle became a flood. It has

39.
Covered punchbowl with swing handles depending from lion masks, made by Benjamin Pyne of London. Leaf tips border the lid and body, which are embellished with zones of concave fluting. English, 1701–2. Height: 45.7 cm. (18 in.). William Rockhill Nelson Gallery of Art and Atkins Museum of Fine Arts, Kansas City, Missouri, gift of Mr. and Mrs. Joseph S. Atha

designer Jean Bérain and the engraver Jean Lepautre. Geometric forms were taken up in other important European cities, along with classical ornamentation; in England, on the other hand, it was more usual for the forms to be left plain.

Toward the end of the seventeenth century, in England and Holland, the lavish naturalistic and floral ornamentation of the baroque style gave place to a new style, commonly called William and Mary since the period of its manufacture coincided approximately with the reign of the two rulers (1689–1702). Repetitive designs, vertical or spiral flutes, gadrooning and classical motifs were all combined to create stately silver (plates 39 and 40) that was only slightly less formal than earlier pieces in the baroque taste.

40.
Detail of armorial on the Benjamin Pyne covered punchbowl (plate 39). The decorative frame for the crest of the Codrington family includes pricked scale decoration, engraved foliage, a matted background and chased outlining of the repoussé areas.

6 The Eighteenth Century: Variations on Classicism

The Queen Anne Style   Toward the end of the seventeenth century supplies of silver in England were no longer sufficient to keep up with increased demand, and for a number of years English goldsmiths had to melt down coins or buy silver illegally from opportunists who amassed bullion by clipping small pieces of silver from coins. The government, unable to stop this practice with stringent laws and penalties, was faced with a great deal of vandalized coinage in circulation and an inability to replace it. An ingenious solution was hit upon: the government passed a law requiring silversmiths to work in silver of a higher standard, the Britannia standard, with only 4.2 percent copper alloy, instead of the 7.5 percent of the sterling standard. The purpose of the law was to encourage people to bring their old plate directly to the mint to provide bullion for a new issue of currency, rather than taking it to silversmiths to be melted down and fashioned into new articles.

The law was called "An Act for the encouragement of wrought plate to be coined," and it came into effect on March 25, 1697. English silversmiths bitterly resented the new ruling, but for the next twenty-two years, until 1719, they had to work in the Britannia standard. The act had the desired effect, although it threw the economy of the goldsmiths into temporary disarray. Their raw material was now softer under the tool and more expensive. In addition to raising their prices, they chose the practical solution of economizing where it was most possible to economize: in the cost of labor. They began fashioning plain forms without decoration. The style developed by these silversmiths came to be known as Queen Anne, although this is something of a misnomer since Anne reigned only from 1702 to 1714, and the style began before her reign and lasted well into that of her successor, George I (1714–27). Nevertheless, the essentials of the style were created in her reign.

Colorplate 11.
The geometric forms of the Queen Anne style were soon adopted in Boston, the most urbane of early colonial towns. John Coney, the maker of this exceptional inkstand, was a leading silversmith of that city. American, c. 1715. Height: 10.7 cm. (4¼ in.). Metropolitan Museum of Art, New York, bequest of Charles Allen Munn, 1924

46.
The ornament on this silver cruet frame is low, whether cast, repoussé or chased. The typically Régence designs on the frame are derived from the earlier vocabulary of French classicism, but they are lighter and more playful. The strapwork, although it is symmetrical, has become lively. Made in Paris by Richard Jarry. French, c. 1717–22. Length: 27.9 cm. (11 in.). Metropolitan Museum of Art, New York, bequest of Catherine D. Wentworth, 1948

Colorplate 12.
As the eighteenth century progressed, ewers and basins were used largely for display purposes. Decorated strapwork interrupted by applied cast and chased medallions containing personifications of the four continents and the liberal arts ornament this silver-gilt ewer and basin. Made in the Régence style by Nicolas Ostertag of Augsburg. German, c. 1730. Diameter of basin: 52.7 cm. (20¾ in.). Height of ewer: 27.3 cm. (10¾ in.). Cooper-Hewitt Museum, gift of the Trustees of the Estate of James Hazen Hyde

metrical relief decoration. Meissonier's work for important patrons like the king of Portugal established the rococo as the new style for people of fashion. Classic motifs still prevailed but were given new expression. Overlapping scales might be wrapped spirally up a form, with leaves and scrolls added to continue the movement (plate 48). Concave fluting, which had been a popular late seventeenth-century decoration, was twisted in spiral fashion (plate 49).

By the 1740s asymmetry had reached rather extraordinarily manic heights, especially in London (plate 50), with such disjunctive motifs as a lion's muzzle and paw, corn, water plants, palm trees, naked babes and infant Mercurys along with waterfalls and shells all thrown together in one composition.

The shell was a common motif in rococo decoration; indeed, the word "rococo" is derived from the French *rocaille*, meaning shell. It was the frilly, fluted edges of shells and their crusty surface textures that were most used in rococo ornament (plate 51).

Even while asymmetrical ornamentation was at its wildest, forms remained stable, and although flat pieces like trays and salvers might have a syncopated outline, heavily applied with cast asymmetrical decoration, the balance was ultimately regulated by equivalent decoration on the opposite side. Underlying much rococo ornament can be seen the noble, stable shapes of the preceding era. On undecorated pieces, the spirit of the age was conveyed by a sinuous profile, or perhaps by handles made up of S- and C-scrolls that curved away from each other before moving toward their juncture with the vessel.

Chinese elements were particularly strong in all the English decorative arts of the rococo period. Sometimes the dragon itself can be seen on silver (colorplate 13), but more often exotic suggestions appear in the form of small Oriental figures occupied in agricultural pursuits

47.
This silver salver or tray is chased and engraved with rococo decoration, the origin of which is clearly discernible in the earlier bandwork of the Régence style. Cast flower, leaf and shell motifs are applied to the edge. Made by Augustine Courtauld of London, possibly for a tripod teapot. English, 1735–6. Height: 15.2 cm. (6 in.). Metropolitan Museum of Art, New York, gift of Irwin Untermyer, 1974

Colorplate 13.
Cast dragons—their tails hinged and extendable to support a dish—are modeled after beasts found on the Oriental lacquer panels that were popular among the upper levels of society in England and France. This decorative and practical brazier was made in London by Charles Frederick Kandler. English, 1742–3. Width: 17.2 cm. (6¾ in.). Metropolitan Museum of Art, New York, bequest of Irwin Untermyer, 1974

Colorplate 14.
The boat shape became popular in the 1750s. This extraordinary silver tureen, its ornamentation a tour de force of sculptural cast and chased work, was crafted by Edmé-Pierre Balzac, one of the leading silversmiths of Paris, for the Duc de Penthièvre. French, 1757–8. Length: 39 cm. (15⅜ in.). Metropolitan Museum of Art, New York, bequest of Catherine D. Wentworth, 1948

52.
Chinoiseries of pagodas and Oriental women bracketed by asymmetrical scrolls—along with floral pendants, shells, a lion mask and paw and scalework—ornament this tea caddy. Made in London by William Cripps. English, 1752–3. Height: 12.7 cm. (5 in.). Cooper-Hewitt Museum, gift of the Trustees of the Estate of James Hazen Hyde

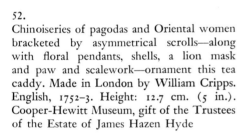

(plate 52). The Oriental influence can also be seen in the pagodalike form of the épergnes, or centerpieces, of the time (plate 53).

A gradual quietening down of the excesses of the rococo is seen in the late 1740s (colorplate 14). By the 1760s, the style had lost most of its sculptural quality and was represented more by low relief or chased and matted surface decoration, in which form it was popular in Scandinavia (plate 54). The selection of motifs narrowed gradually to shellwork, flowers and leaves (plate 55). A rather unimaginative form of rococo was still being produced in the 1770s for the conservative public, but the work had become crude and curiously lifeless.

In America, the extremes of the style were never adopted, although they were undoubtedly imported for certain customers. The rococo was seen especially in the decoration of teapot spouts, handles, engraved armorials that appeared surrounded by ornament on salvers, trays and tankards (plate 56), and in the profiles of mugs, teapots and coffeepots. The time lag that had been noticeable between London and colonial fashions in the seventeenth century had now closed (plate 57).

53

53.
The finial in the shape of a pineapple, a symbol of hospitality, and the palm tree trunks and canopy are exotic touches on this épergne. The baskets are ajouré with cast and applied floral decoration. Made in London by Thomas Heming. English, 1766–7. Height: 62.2 cm. (24½ in.). Metropolitan Museum of Art, New York, gift of Lewis Einstein, 1952

54.
The beaker remained a favorite shape in Scandinavia, where the rococo decoration was generally confined to light engraving or wriggle work with shells and scrolls. Owners often had their initials engraved on these tall cups. The maker of this beaker was Isak Sauer of Stockholm. Swedish, 1760. Height: 17.8 cm. (7 in.). Cooper-Hewitt Museum, anonymous gift

55.
This whimsical teapot, shaped like a melon with a spout like a vine stem, is a charming example of late rococo. It was made in The Hague by the unknown master E.E. Dutch, 1765. New handle added c. 1900. Height: 13.3 cm. (5¼ in.). Metropolitan Museum of Art, New York, bequest of Alfred Duane Pell, 1925

56.
Several decades of Massachusetts tankards were characterized by decorative devices such as the median band, five-stepped lid, acorn finial and molded base band. The new element displayed in this tankard is the lightly engraved rococo scrolling around the initials. Made by a Boston master, Samuel Minott. American, c. 1750. Height: 21.6 cm. (8½ in.). Smithsonian Institution, National Museum of American History (National Museum of History and Technology)

54

55

57

57.
Although the decorative motifs of this delicate ajouré silver cake basket are drawn from the rococo style, the symmetry presages the early influence of the neoclassical style. Made in New York by Myer Myers. American, c. 1765. Length: 36.5 cm. (14½ in.). Metropolitan Museum of Art, New York, Morris K. Jessup Fund, 1954

56

Neoclassicism During the 1740s, while the rococo was at its height, excavations were under way in Italy at two Roman cities, Pompeii and Herculaneum. A decade later, in the 1750s, the Greek colony of Paestum, also in Italy, was excavated. All three cities had been important in the ancient world, and the significance of their discoveries was not lost on the polite world of the eighteenth century, where a classical education was still considered the only education. At first only savants and archaeological enthusiasts were interested in supporting the excavations, but the publication of books on the discoveries opened up the subject to a more general public. The most important work was also the most general and didactic: J. J. Winckelmann's *History of the Art of Antiquity*, which was published in Germany in 1764. Winckelmann pronounced the superiority of Greek art over Roman and confirmed a burgeoning craze for things Greek.

The "Greek taste" appeared in clothes, hairstyles and, more seriously, in architecture. The first silver in the Greek taste appeared in the 1760s (plate 58), although for some time many pieces showed only

58.
Robert-Joseph Auguste, a celebrated Parisian goldsmith, no doubt referred to the illustrations in one of the new books on antiquities in designing these candelabra in the early neoclassical—or "Greek taste"—style. French, 1767–8. Height: 37.5 cm. (14¾ in.). Metropolitan Museum of Art, New York, bequest of Catherine D. Wentworth, 1948

a partial adoption of motifs (plate 59). The craze was encouraged by a waning interest in the rococo, along with a groundswell led against it by such architects as Jacques-François Blondel in France and Robert Adam in England. After four years in Italy, Adam had come back to England in 1758 convinced of the purity of the classical world and ultimately its appropriateness to the arts. His book *The Works in Architecture* was not published until 1773, however, and although he promoted neoclassicism while he was architect to George III, it was in France that the new taste was pioneered in a more public way (plate 60).

The early French neoclassical silver shows a delicacy in its selection of motifs, even when the object itself is imposing in proportions and static in appearance. A similar refinement and attempt at authenticity can be seen in contemporary silver from England (plate 61). The attractiveness of these pieces is perhaps a result of their having been based not on massive architectural remains but on actual classical domestic objects, made originally in bronze, pottery, pewter or some

59.
Neoclassical details on this silver hot water urn are the high beading on the handles (see plate 3), convex fluting and acanthus leaf decoration on the spigot. Made by Auguste Le Sage in London. English, 1770–71. Height: 22 cm. (8½ in.). Cooper-Hewitt Museum, anonymous gift

60

61

60.
This stately tureen and stand, ordered by Catherine the Great of Russia as part of a huge service plate for her favorite, Count Orloff, is an imposing example of the seriousness with which classical taste was advanced. It is not a copy of an antique object, but a French tureen embellished with a total covering of classical motifs in the Greek taste. Made in Paris by Jacques-Nicolas Roettiers. French, 1770–71. Height of tureen: 27.9 cm. (11 in.). Diameter of stand: 46.6 cm. (18⅜ in.). Metropolitan Museum of Art, New York, Rogers Fund, 1933

61.
Carefully planned classical touches on this utilitarian tripod dishstand include rosetted guilloche decorating the ring, convex gadroons on the lamp holder, fully modeled rams' heads on the sliders and rams' legs to hold up the extremities of the arms. The arms of the dishstand are adjustable. Made in London by Septimus and James Crespel. English, 1770–71. Width: 35.6 cm. (14 in.). Metropolitan Museum of Art, New York, gift of Madame Lilliana Teruzzi, 1966

62.
Robert Adam may have provided Matthew Boulton with the design for this silver stand and spirit burner. The piece demonstrates a seriousness of purpose in creating a wonderful modern object by using entirely classical motifs. Made in Birmingham by Matthew Boulton. English, 1775–6. Height: 12.7 cm. (5 in.). Metropolitan Museum of Art, New York, gift of Madame Lilliana Teruzzi, 1966

other material, so that an idea of suitable proportion was implicit in the source for the new designs (plate 62). By the 1780s the essentials of Adam's preferences were established as *the* mode for domestic silver (plate 63). Delicate motifs associated with the early imperial cities of Pompeii and Herculaneum (rather than with the truly Greek city of earlier date at Paestum)—guilloche, twisted tape decoration, paterae, small rosettes, palmettes, husks and festoons of small flowers, Greek key and fret ornament, and severed rams' heads and masks, usually in relief—are the ones found on Adamesque and Adam-inspired silver. Normally these decorations are in flatwork—engraved or bright-cut or ajouré (plate 64)—so that nothing interferes with the profile of the vessel, which has the clean lines of a classical vase (plate 65). Although neoclassical allusions to Greek and Roman models were often obvious, a plainer yet no less effective style, deriving from the classical vocabulary, also evolved (plate 66).

By the 1790s the neoclassical style had been in vogue for over twenty years and could almost take itself for granted. No longer was it necessary for silversmiths to make an effort to stay close to classical models. The slight pricked and bright-cut decoration of the time was in no way derived from Greek or Roman artifacts or their decoration.

62

63.
A faithfulness to Greek models can be seen in the rim decoration and the ornament surrounding the armorial center of this early neoclassical silver tray by John Carter of London. English, 1775–6. Diameter: 51.4 cm. (20¼ in.). Metropolitan Museum of Art, New York, bequest of Ogden Livingston Mills, 1937

64.
Vitruvian scrolls, beading and rosettes set within circles stand out on the pierced ground of this boat-shaped sugar bowl. The bowl stands on an oval foot, somewhat pointed, a common shape for both bases and containers in the last decades of the century in England. The dark blue glass liner is contemporary. Made in London by Robert Hennell. English, 1783–4. Width: 15.2 cm. (6 in.). Metropolitan Museum of Art, New York, Rogers Fund, 1911

64

65.
Plainer domestic silver, which nevertheless followed contemporary lines, was made outside the great centers of Paris and London. The finial of this urn-shaped sugar bowl suggests the form of a Greek kylix. Made by the unidentified maker M.H.P. in Oporto. Portuguese, c. 1780–90. Height: 21.6 cm. (8½ in.). Metropolitan Museum of Art, New York, Rogers Fund, 1912

66.
The repetition of fine concave fluting is characteristic of the last decade of the eighteenth century, when silver was very light and graceful. This candelabrum can be converted into a single candlestick by removing the candle arms from the central shaft. By the unidentified maker H.S.R. in Lisbon. Portuguese, c. 1790. Height: 36.8 cm. (14½ in.). Metropolitan Museum of Art, New York, Rogers Fund, 1912

65

66

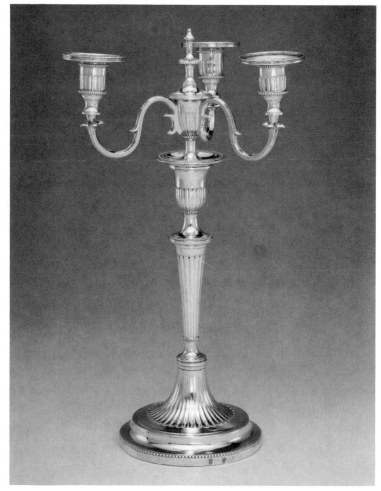

This late neoclassical style can be seen in the work of Paul Revere (1735–1818), America's most famous silversmith. The pleasing quality of the pieces in his tea set (colorplate 15) reminds us that of all styles, America's taste seems most at home with a classical line, just as the English preference seems to be innately expressed by the Queen Anne style and the French by a formality most clearly seen in the art of the age of Louis XIV—preferences that may stem from the styles being associated with periods of great national success.

After the upheaval of the French Revolution of 1789, when much silver was sent to the melting pot and the guilds were disbanded, French silversmiths were once again free to return to their art. They were also released from working in the high standard, with only 4.2 percent alloy, and permitted to work in a much lower standard, having 20 percent alloy, if they chose. Yet the Revolution had jarred the economy of the nation and removed many of the silversmiths' customers. Probably because of the shortage of money, silver was less substantial than it had ever been. The shapes were elegant, but the decoration was often made separately and soldered or bolted onto the surface, rather than being cast or repoussé.

If archaeology was the origin of the neoclassical style, politics kept it going, at any rate in France. The notion of an all-powerful monarchy and aristocracy was offensive to the Revolutionary state of mind—it was un-Greek. During the succeeding brief republic, the Directoire (1795–1804), a return to the Greek taste was the order of the day. But instead of the abstract and formal use of Greek motifs that had been characteristic of the early neoclassicism, figures and personalities such as gods and heroes became the focal point of decoration. An unexpected part of the ancient world, Egypt, also provided decorative motifs. In 1802 Dominique Vivant Denon, a soldier-archaeologist who had accompanied Napoleon during his Egyptian campaign in 1798–9, published his *Journeys in Upper and Lower Egypt*. The book of travels was profusely illustrated and proved the inspiration for entire Egyptian interiors with specially designed Egyptian furniture. On silver, such features were restricted to applied cast sphinx heads, somewhat Egyptianized palmettes, and capitals of the water-leaf type—all used in combination with contemporary and quite un-Egyptian forms.

In 1804, Napoleon abolished the Directoire and was proclaimed First Consul. Shortly thereafter he crowned himself emperor. Charles Percier and Pierre-François-Léonard Fontaine, two architects with strongly classical enthusiasms, were given the commission for furnishing Napoleon's state apartments, which set the seal of imperial approval on the continuation of the neoclassical. Indeed, it would have been an awkward moment to have abandoned the classical mode, with all its allusions to the power of past civilization, for Napoleon was intent

Colorplate 15.
After the American Revolution, which had held back the earlier phases of the neoclassical style in the colonies, Americans delighted in silver characterized by oval forms, concave flutes, lightly engraved decoration and an overall delicacy. This silver tea set in the late neoclassical style was made by Paul Revere. Boston, c. 1790. Height of tea caddy: 23.5 cm. (9¼ in.). Metropolitan Museum of Art, New York, bequest of A. T. Clearwater, 1933

Colorplate 16.
With ram's-head spouts, serpent handles and winged lion feet, this pair of sauceboats serves as a superb example of the fully developed neoclassical style in the United States. The maker, Anthony Rasch, was trained in Europe. Philadelphia, c. 1810. Length: 28.6 cm. (11¼ in.). Metropolitan Museum of Art, New York, Fletcher Fund, 1959

70.
William Shepherd adopted the Roman sarcophagus form for the body of this silver sauce tureen, one of a pair, supported on four ball feet and adorned with a cast finial and rams' heads holding ring handles. London, 1804–5. Length: 17.8 cm. (7 in.). Metropolitan Museum of Art, New York, bequest of Ogden Livingston Mills, 1937

Instead, there was a greater attempt at archaeological accuracy (plates 69 and 70). Vivant Denon's work on Egyptian antiquities was known in England, and some sphinxes and water leaves appeared, although the influence was less prominent in silver than in furniture.

The neoclassical style was firmly established throughout the Continent and England. It penetrated to Russia, where extremely elegant services were made for the court, and it was warmly accepted in America (colorplate 16). The style had a long duration, something over sixty years; other styles introduced during the period, such as the Egyptian craze, were ephemeral by comparison.

7   The Nineteenth Century: Eclipse of the Craftsman

The word "industrial" had a very somber connotation for goldsmiths and silversmiths in the nineteenth century, especially in England and France, where controls on the production of wares had been strictest. The very restraints that had served to keep standards of craftsmanship and design uniformly high were now removed by legislation. In England, the Apprenticeship Act was repealed in 1814. This weakened the guild system by divesting it of the right to bar unqualified makers from selling their wares; it also legitimized the activities of the industrial firms in the Midland cities of Manchester, Sheffield and Birmingham, where mass production of a sort had been in existence for some decades. Two years later, in 1816, England officially adopted the gold standard. Henceforth there was less concern for protecting the country's silver currency, and authorities could afford to turn a blind eye to the production of Sheffield plate (copper plated with a thin surface of silver) in the Midlands. The gold standard was adopted in most European countries during the course of the century; Russia was the last to do so in 1897. In these countries, too, a relaxation of controls on the use of silver accompanied the change.

During the third decade of the nineteenth century, in the three countries that would be most active in silver production—France, England and the United States—evolving conditions gave handwrought and manufactured plate equal status in the marketplace. In effect this could only favor the one and menace the other, for handwrought plate was much more expensive to produce but not visibly very different from a factory-made piece. The result was that by 1830 many independent silversmiths had either retired, gone bankrupt, or adopted, so far as they could, the labor-saving methods of industry. Only a handful of boys entered into apprenticeship, which had become voluntary, and few were the new makers' marks registered at guild headquarters.

Colorplate 17.
This Scottish cup, or *cawg*, is an interpretation in silver, ivory and ebony of a traditional wooden drinking vessel with lug handles. It is an early manifestation of the romanticizing of the past that was reflected in the poems and novels of such authors as Sir Walter Scott. Inscribed: *The Gift of AS to her Grandson RS 1789*. By an unknown maker. Probably Edinburgh. Height: 9.5 cm. (3¾ in.). Cooper-Hewitt Museum, anonymous gift

In questions of taste, design and the invention of new styles, the initiative now passed to the manufacturers, for there was no longer a court- and aristocracy-oriented craft from which lesser and provincial makers could take their lead. Interest in the neoclassical was nearly exhausted by about 1830; the style had come to be relegated to use for official and "safe" taste. What was new beginning in 1830 were naturalism (plate 71)—the use of carefully observed and re-created plant and leaf forms as decoration—and the Gothic, a general taste encouraged by trends in literature, which found expression in architecture, interiors, furniture and fashion. At first, Gothic silver simply consisted of pieces redolent with medieval associations, such as goblets (plate 72), medievally attired figures around the bases of large works or sentimental folk pieces made in precious materials (colorplate 17).

There was also a quite unselfconscious reintroduction of discarded styles from the past (colorplate 18), the rococo being a particularly popular revival. The less expensive manufactured plate could be afforded by a clientele drawn from a far wider social and economic group, and advanced styles, it was assumed, would be too precarious to offer as main fare; safer to keep to traditional styles, however liberally interpreted. It was this need that encouraged what has been variously dubbed eclecticism, historicism or pure mishmash.

In 1851 the Great Exhibition was held in the Crystal Palace in London, marking the celebration of England's and Europe's recovery from the economic consequences of the Napoleonic Wars and from some of the social and political dislocations due to industrialization. All nations were invited to display their agricultural inventions, transportation innovations, medical equipment, industrial goods and decorative arts. To judge from reviews of the entries in the silver category, tastefulness and novelty were the most admired. "Tastefulness" appears to mean the presence of features that had been sanctified by age and that, by extension, lent a certain cachet to the object—for instance, fully modeled figures of animals or people engaged in praiseworthy activities such as hunting, battling the Saracen or enacting some episode from classical mythology. If tastefulness seems to us a baffling criterion, we should remember that the subject matter of such decoration presupposed a liberal education on the part of the maker or the owner (or both), which in turn suggested gentility and hence acceptability.

The other term of approbation, "novelty," also needs clarification. As the illustrations in the catalogue of the exhibition show, contemporary taste most admired novel pieces in which decorative details adopted from earlier styles were disjunctively or intricately recombined rather than tamely set forth. What contemporary critics could not see (though so very apparent to us now) was that the evolution taking place was not one of decoration but of form—yet a form so well conceived that any decoration could be applied without overwhelming it (plates 73–77).

72.
The intention of this piece is Gothic, the goblet being reminiscent of the romance of medieval chivalry. Nevertheless the decorative fluting and die-pressed ivy band are contemporary motifs, and the thistle shape dates back only to the sixteenth century. Made in London by Samuel Hennell. English, 1814–15. Height: 15.9 cm. (6¼ in.). Metropolitan Museum of Art, New York, gift of Julian Clarence Levi, 1966

73.
The shape of this hot water urn, with its extremely wide top, is a form that evolved gradually during the 1820s. The square plinth on ball feet, lions' masks supporting handles and convex fluting around the lower body all mark the survival of neoclassical taste. Made in London by John Angell. English, 1830–31. Height: 34.9 cm. (13¾ in.). Metropolitan Museum of Art, New York, gift of Madame Lilliana Teruzzi, 1966

72

73

74

75

74.
The neoclassical winged lions on paw feet, scrolled handles and sarcophagus shape of this basket recall features of an earlier style. Nevertheless the handles, which are continuous with the widely extended rim, and the die-pressed rose blossoms of the lower frieze give the piece a contemporary appearance. Made by Fletcher and Gardiner in Philadelphia. American, c. 1830. Length: 39.7 cm. (15⅝ in.). Smithsonian Institution, National Museum of American History (National Museum of History and Technology), gift of Mrs. S. E. Cummings

75.
Although this wine cooler is still wide at the top, the transition from the body to the rim is much less abrupt than in pieces from just a decade earlier. Decoration consists of applied rococo ornament. Made, probably by John Watson, in Sheffield. English, 1838–9. Height: 28.6 cm. (11¼ in.). Metropolitan Museum of Art, New York, gift of Mrs. Margaret Carney, from the Estate of Farrell Joseph Carney, Elphin, County Roscommon, Eire, 1979

Colorplate 19.
The original model of this claret jug was entered in the Great Exhibition of 1851, held at the Crystal Palace in London, but the design was kept in production for several years afterward. Decorated with whimsical allusions to wine harvesting, the jug is suggestive of a Gothic form. Made in London by Joseph Angell III. English, 1854–5. Height: 31.5 cm. (12¼ in.). Cooper-Hewitt Museum, gift of Louise B. Scott

76.
Silver rattles decorated with bells and terminating in a branch of coral or ivory for teething were common toys for children of upper-class families in the nineteenth century. This example includes a whistle on the end opposite the coral teether. The metal parts of the rattle would have been pressed in a die and carefully seamed with solder. Made in the neo-rococo taste, probably in Birmingham. English, c. 1835–40. Length: 17.7 cm. (7 in.). Cooper-Hewitt Museum, gift of Mrs. Max Farrand

77.
Inspiration for the Oriental motifs on this tea set was drawn from rococo silver of a century earlier. The fully globular form illustrates another stage in the continuing evolution of line and shape that occurred approximately each decade in the nineteenth century. Made by Bailey and Co., Philadelphia. American, c. 1845–50. Height of urn: 40 cm. (15¾ in.). Smithsonian Institution, National Museum of American History (National Museum of History and Technology), bequest of Marion Leigh Wells

76

77

One of the quieter notes struck amid the generally robust styles of the midcentury (colorplate 19)—and one that has been little noticed or written about—was that of the pastoral and rustic world. Plain silver in the style of the eighteenth century was also revived, although decorated with repoussé designs that are not a duplication of eighteenth-century work and are, moreover, often inconsistent with the form of the piece (plates 78 and 79).

Both before and after the Great Exhibition there was much debate as to what art might lie in an industrially produced object—a difficulty that never would have occurred to the eighteenth-century mind. In the decade following the 1851 exhibition, although designs in the opulent taste of the preceding decade were continued by many manufacturers, projecting ornamentation was replaced by a smoother version (plate 80). Repoussé and cast work were out and engraved work was in. Only handles and finials retained some of the boisterousness of the preceding age. This switch to a quieter note was possibly the result of the high regard for the French entries in the exhibition (colorplate 20). Restraint became synonymous with good taste.

A number of events strongly affected the design and use of silver in the second part of the nineteenth century. The first of these was the franchising of the electroplating method patented by Elkington's

78.
This beaker, of traditional Swedish form, has the remains of wheel-made wriggle work around the top. The remaining decoration, a mixture of chased and repoussé rococo and seventeenth-century motifs, was added later, probably in the 1840s. Made in Bergen by Jørgen Greve. Norwegian, c. 1770. Height: 17.4 cm. (6⅞ in.). Cooper-Hewitt Museum, gift of the Misses Hewitt

79

79.
Originally a plain neoclassical set from about 1800, this teapot and stand were inappropriately redecorated with chased and repoussé chinoiseries and rococo scrolls, probably in the 1840s when such motifs were again popular. Made in London by Henry Chawner. English, c. 1800. Height of teapot: 14 cm. (5½ in.). Width of tray: 12.3 cm. (4¾ in.). Cooper-Hewitt Museum, gift of the Misses Hewitt

Colorplate 20.
Classical taste is reflected in the somewhat mannered double palmette frieze and the shallow convex fluting of this claret jug. Designed by Constant Sevin and made by Desiré Attarge for the firm of F. Barbedienne, Paris. French, 1875. Height: 29.2 cm. (11½ in.). Metropolitan Museum of Art, New York, Rogers Fund, 1969

83.
Wager cups were so named because in order to win the wager one had to drink both cups dry before setting the vessel down. The skirt of the figure forms the large cup; a second cup swings on pivots above the cast body. Made by an unknown master, probably of Nuremberg. German, c. 1885. Height: 35.6 cm. (14 in.). Metropolitan Museum of Art, New York, bequest of Martha A. Zales, 1978

Colorplate 21.
Although Tiffany's called the design of this teapot Saracenic, it is easier to see it as a revival of the sarcophagus shape of the late neoclassical period. The silver enamel pot is topped with an ivory finial. Designed by Edward C. Moore, Jr., for the New York firm. American, c. 1878. Length: 27.9 cm. (11 in.). Metropolitan Museum of Art, New York, gift of a friend of the Museum, 1897

silver within the range of all but the most humble, and a great many small pieces were made—book markers, bouquet holders, all manner of little decorative spoons and such items as tea balls, wine labels and menu holders—that could be bought quite cheaply. The stately procession of tea and coffee services continued (plate 81), whereas the use of dinner services tended to decline. The stupendous Mackay service made by Tiffany & Company in 1877 and 1878 was a notable exception to the trend. John Mackay was the owner of the Comstock Bonanza, the richest part of the famous Comstock Lode. He was already wealthy, but the wealth that flowed from this mine made him one of the richest men in America after 1873, the year of its discovery. From this very mine, silver was delivered to Tiffany's, which made it into the most famous and most traveled dinner service of the century. The dinner and dessert service for twenty persons consisted of well over a thousand pieces and was a central part of Mrs. Mackay's notable hospitality in Paris and London for twenty-five years.

The quickening of the silver trade in America is well illustrated by the rise of Tiffany & Company. In 1847, Tiffany's began selling small silver wares, many made abroad. Soon the firm engaged a designer, Gustav Herter, whose designs were carried out by independent New York silversmiths and retailed by Tiffany's. In 1851, Edward C. Moore, Jr., a silversmith and designer of genius, joined the company; within little more than five years the company had become the leading producer of new designs for New York society (frontispiece, plate 82 and colorplate 21). The fruitful association between Tiffany's and Moore would last for over forty years.

84.
Although this historical re-creation is close to seventeenth-century tankards, one can discern a false note in the use of the same cast lion figure for both the feet and the thumb piece. Made in Copenhagen by A. F. Stephanssen. Danish, c. 1900. Height: 15.2 cm. (6 in.). Metropolitan Museum of Art, New York, bequest of A. T. Clearwater, 1933

During the last twenty years of the century neoclassical wares reminiscent of Paul Revere's were popular in America, and in England Queen Anne tea sets were favored. In Germany, trick drinking vessels such as the wager cup, which had been popular in the seventeenth century, were produced (plate 83), while the Scandinavian countries made a strong showing with capacious tankards (plate 84), and Holland turned out beakers with windmills on their bases. But apart from these and other accurate re-creations, manufactured plate was bereft of new ideas. There was little to do but go the rounds again of the exotic historic styles (plates 85 and 86 and colorplate 22), from rococo to Louis XVI to Régence to Henri II. The evolution of line or form underlying the decoration continued, however, and roughly each decade a new shape emerged (plate 87).

Toward the end of the century there were two new departures in the arts, the Arts and Crafts movement in England and the Art Nouveau movement in France. The first of these, the Arts and Crafts movement, had a long incubation period. There were in the nineteenth century two attitudes toward solving the vexing problem "What is art in an industrially made article?" Manufacturers had simply assumed that what had been admired and used by the aristocracy and gentry of the past was art now. So they embellished their wares with sculptures, pictorial and realistic ornament and details culled from the past. But

Colorplate 22.
From Liberty's "Cymric" line, this spoon was designed by Archibald Knox to commemorate the coronation of Edward VII in 1901. Mottled enamels and interlaced designs are polite Edwardian interpretations of the Welsh past. English, 1902. Length: 20.3 cm. (8 in.). Metropolitan Museum of Art, New York, gift of Andrew Crispo, 1979

88

89

88.
Designed by C. R. Ashbee and made at the Guild and School of Handicrafts, in Mile End, London, the design of this sugar bowl, with some marks of the planishing hammer deliberately left, stresses that it has been handmade. The springy appearance of the wire handles also gives the feeling that they have been curved manually rather than cast or stamped in a machine. English, 1902–3. Width: 27.3 cm. (10¾ in.). Metropolitan Museum of Art, New York, gift of the Friends of Twentieth-Century Decorative Arts, 1979

89.
Typical of work from the Kalo Workshop in Park Ridge, Illinois, this sugar bowl and creamer are simple in outline, relying for their aesthetic effect on the obvious substantial thickness of the metal and the marks of the planishing hammer. Semiprecious stones ornament the handles. Designed by Clara Barck Welles. American, c. 1905–20. Height: 5.4 cm. (2⅛ in.). Chicago Historical Society

a second school of thought, led by William Morris, held that the machine required only automatic work by an operator in dehumanized conditions. In an attempt to return to the fraternity, knowledge and communal experience that the guild members in the pre-Renaissance period had shared, they established workshops where craftsmen lived in close social confines. As it affected silver, the movement came rather late. Workers had to be found who could between them recover the almost lost techniques of the old gold- and silversmiths, and it was not until the 1880s that any silver emerged from these shops. The influential architect and writer C. R. Ashbee founded his Guild and School of Handicrafts in 1888 at Toynbee Hall in London's East End (plate 88). Similar workshops were established in America; one of the best known, the Kalo Workshop founded by Clara Barck Welles in Park Ridge, Illinois, with a showroom in Chicago, sprang directly from a visit Ashbee made to Chicago in 1900 (plate 89).

Like the Arts and Crafts movement in England, with which it had some affinities, Art Nouveau began with a group of artists, sculptors, painters and designers who were pioneering a new mode in the fine arts. In the decorative arts, this implied a dissatisfaction with industrial forms—an attitude that displayed itself in an almost salacious sensuousness in the use of materials, which proved especially suitable to silver.

90

90.
The characteristic line of the Art Nouveau style can be seen in the tight curve at the high point of the handles of this jardiniere. Made by A. Mayer Söhne. German, c. 1905. Height: 21.6 cm. (8½ in.). Cooper-Hewitt Museum, gift of Ely Jacques Kahn

91

91.
This bonbon dish has the characteristic whiplash curve of the Art Nouveau style in its repoussé decoration, although it is called "Cymric" by the manufacturer and retailer, Liberty's of London. Made in Birmingham for Liberty's, 1902. Height: 6.5 cm. (2½ in.). Cooper-Hewitt Museum, anonymous gift

The Art Nouveau was a very feminine style, and is sometimes explained as a mixture of rococo and Japanese influences—asymmetry from the rococo and the use of natural forms such as trees, flowers and fish from the Japanese. The one undeviating convention of the Art Nouveau style is a long line with a quick curve, now commonly described as the whiplash (plates 90 and 91). This line is seen neither in nature nor in the rococo, nor is it characteristic of Japanese art. It is, rather, an example of a feature that seems to appear at a given time as the visual equivalent of some generally felt mood or attitude. The Art Nouveau was taken up by manufacturers, who continued to use it until the outbreak of World War I.

8 Silver in the Twentieth Century

During the early twentieth century the question of what role art should play in an industrially made object seemed at last to be satisfactorily answered. Quite simply, it was decided that industrially made objects—whether designed by an artist or an industrial designer—should be visibly and obviously the products of the machine, rather than machine imitations of handwork.

Silver produced up to the beginning of World War II is best understood when separated into craft silver and commercial silver. For the most part, the craft studios and craftsmen worked with a number of different materials, not just silver, and their creations are in minute supply compared to those of the industrial companies. Industrial designers continued to make what the public wanted in the way of traditional styles, modified to suit the contemporary eye (plate 92), and also imitations of the styles developed by the small workshops, studios and schools that created handmade silver.

The Wiener Werkstätte, or Vienna Workshops, which lasted from 1903 to 1932, grew out of direct contacts between C. R. Ashbee and Josef Hoffmann, an Austrian architect and painter who brought exhibits from Ashbee's Guild and School of Handicrafts along with handmade works from Scotland and Belgium to the Sezession Exhibition in Vienna of 1900. The aim of the Vienna Workshops was to recover good standards of craftsmanship and to use materials in a natural way to create objects for interior furnishings and jewelry. At first the productions were made in an uncompromisingly geometric—indeed, rectilinear—style deriving from Hoffmann's views on architecture (plate 93). After the arrival of Eduard Wimmer in 1908 (plate 94), however, and increasingly after Dagobert Peche joined the group, a more natural style was adopted that was at once both naturalistic and fanciful (plate 95). Commercial manufacturers, inspired by the products of the

Colorplate 23.
This parcel-gilt bowl by Jean Puiforcat appears to have been inspired by the ancient Chinese bronze vessel called the *tou*, but is typical of its time in the very hard, almost lathe-turned lines. It is a reminder, being in mint condition, of how dramatic parcel-gilt is when fresh. Paris, c. 1930–35. Height: 25 cm. (9⅞ in.). Metropolitan Museum of Art, New York, Edgar Kaufmann, Jr., Gift Fund, 1972

92.
A historical decorative technique, ajouré, and an old form, the tazza, both in vogue in the late seventeenth and early eighteenth centuries, were used to create this early twentieth-century cakestand. Probably made by Dominick and Haff and Company, Newark or New York. American, c. 1900–1910. Height: 13.2 cm. (5 in.). Cooper-Hewitt Museum, anonymous gift

Vienna Workshops, copied their designs, especially in the more fantastic style, but with a time lag of about ten years.

For a brief period following World War I there was a school of design in Germany that sought to unite all the crafts for furnishing and creating a proper human environment under the aegis of architecture. This was the famous Bauhaus, which started in Weimar in 1919, moved to Dessau in 1925, to Berlin in 1932 and disbanded there a year later, in 1933. Although it was constantly under political attack in Germany, the Bauhaus achieved a lasting influence through the work of its founders and students. Professors researched and taught the principles of aesthetics—whether applied to architecture, sculpture and painting or metalwork and ceramics—while trained artisans in properly equipped workshops instructed students in the practical considerations and methods required to turn their designs into finished objects.

Designers trained at the Bauhaus at first tried to work intuitively, and in no particular style; later they were profoundly influenced by the

93.
Silver basket designed by Josef Hoffmann
and made in the Wiener Werkstätte (Vienna
Workshops). Austrian, 1905. Height: 24.1
cm. (9½ in.). Metropolitan Museum of Art,
New York, Rogers Fund, 1970

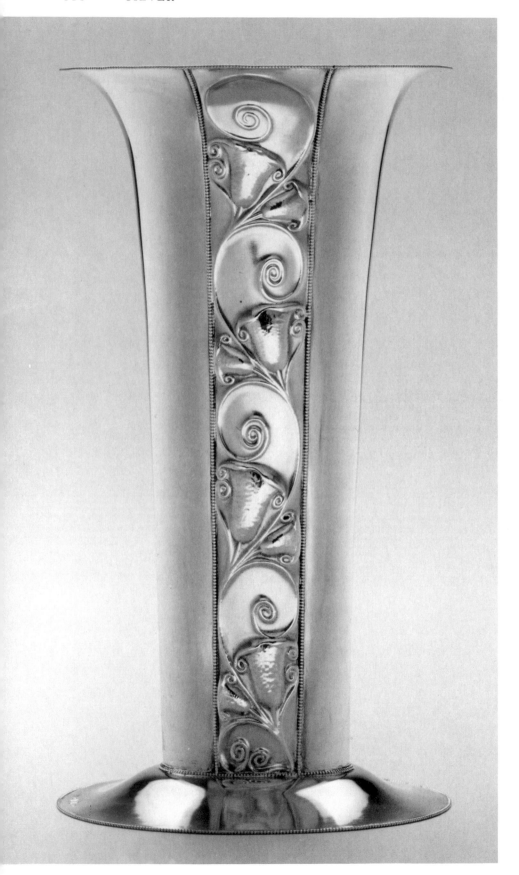

94.
This silver-gilt vase was handmade by Josef Hoffmann in the more naturalistic style apparent in the Wiener Werkstätte's designs after 1908. The oval, trumpet-shaped vase has a vertical panel set off by beaded edges containing repoussé convolvulus blossoms. Austrian, c. 1908–10. Height: 23.2 cm. (9⅛ in.). Metropolitan Museum of Art, New York, Edward C. Moore, Jr., gift fund, 1923

95.
The fluid, highly decorative work produced by the Wiener Werkstätte during its late period can be seen in this silver vase made by Dagobert Peche. Austrian, c. 1920. Height: 23.9 cm. (9⅜ in.). Cooper-Hewitt Museum, gift of Ely Jacques Kahn

arrival of the Dutch constructivist Theo van Doesburg and the Hungarian László Moholy-Nagy. Thereafter the aim, especially in the metalworking shop, was to specify almost exclusively geometric forms, with an eye to making such designs easy and natural for machine production. These Bauhaus pieces were copied by some commercial silver producers but were never particularly popular; the style is occasionally seen in a somewhat debased form in pieces from the 1930s and 1940s.

After World War I a style came to the fore in France which, while relying upon geometric forms, was more delicate and lively than that of the Bauhaus. This was Art Moderne, now known as Art Deco, which affected all forms of personal style and furnishings, including

96.
The standard ingredients of the Art Deco
style—angularity, symmetricality and verti-
cality—can be seen in this coffee service
made in Copenhagen for Georg Jensen in
about 1935 from a design by Sigvard Berna-
dotte. Height: 18.4 cm. (7¼ in.). Metropolitan Museum of Art, New York, Edward
C. Moore, Jr., gift fund, 1939

97.
Twentieth-century streamlining has been applied to a classic Greek pottery shape in this dish from the Borgila Studio in Stockholm. The decorative touch where the handles meet the rim of the bowl is a modern borrowing from the vocabulary of structural engineering. Made from a design by Erik Fleming. Swedish, 1932. Width: 24.1 cm. (9½ in.). Metropolitan Museum of Art, New York, Edward C. Moore, Jr., gift fund, 1934

silver (plate 96 and colorplate 23). From the time of the Paris Exposition Internationale des Arts Décoratifs et Industriels Modernes in 1925 until the eve of World War II, Art Deco was the reigning style, although its chic angularity (plate 98) was softened in the three or four years before 1940. Most of this period was one of severe economic distress in England, Europe and America, and the market for silver was greatly reduced.

After World War II it became quickly apparent that very fine industrial goods were emerging from Scandinavia. They were extraordinarily well made, with no sense of difficulty between the personality of a handmade object and the lifeless quality of a machine-made one. The groundwork for this success had been laid in the interwar period, and although Norway and Denmark, and to some extent Finland, suffered in World War II, they all partook, along with Sweden, in the extraordinary renaissance of Scandinavian design and industry immediately after the end of hostilities. A number of private studios had been active before the war. It was in these that the twentieth-century style—that subtle quality that distinguishes one age from another—could first be discerned. Silversmiths began to make products

9   Advice for the Collector

The fact that silver is intrinsically valuable is a plus for even modest collectors. Unlike most other collectibles, silver antiques consistently rise in value with the rise in the price of the metal and the advance in the antique market itself. There is, however, a potential snare to silver collecting, since prices are often higher than either the condition of an object or its actual age would merit, and unwary collectors may find they are paying too much for their purchases. The reproductions of the last twenty years of the nineteenth century constitute a special danger to collectors concentrating on earlier periods. In order to be certain that they are buying objects as old as their styles claim (colorplate 24) and not later re-creations, collectors must be careful to acquaint themselves with the marks, methods of manufacture, styles and current prices of a chosen field. For this, attendance at sales rooms affords an opportunity to examine silver at first hand; and given advance notice, many museums will allow access to objects not on exhibition. A careful, leisurely examination of any family silver also provides valuable knowledge and familiarity.

There are many ways to approach silver collecting. Some people prefer to concentrate on a single object, such as spoons, mustard pots or candlesticks; others select a single period, such as the neoclassic, rococo or early Victorian. But perhaps the greatest challenge arises in choosing as one's focus an area that has as yet received little attention— for instance, the naturalistic wares of the early nineteenth century, or the works of little known silversmiths operating in the United States, especially the Northeast, between about 1830 and 1870. This brings the reward of establishing a body of work that may pose new questions for scholars and perhaps even push forward knowledge of the history of silver manufacture.

Collecting photographs is an excellent method of establishing a detailed body of information, amplifying the terse generalizations made

Colorplate 24.
Record prices are received for rare silver if, in addition to good condition and respectable age, the object has historical interest. Before committing large sums for acquisition, collectors must be especially careful to judge whether such pieces have the right shape, weight, dimensions, decoration and marks for the period claimed. These qualifications are certainly met by this American colonial silver chocolate pot by Edward Winslow, a member of the first generation of American-born and American-trained silversmiths active in Boston. American, late seventeenth–early eighteenth century. Height: 23.2 cm. (9⅛ in.). Metropolitan Museum of Art, New York, bequest of A. T. Clearwater, 1933

in reference books. Art periodicals, sales catalogues and dealers' advertisements contribute free photographic material that quickly becomes an invaluable reference tool of one's own making.

Hallmarks   From the fifth century onward in the Eastern Roman Empire, marks denoting the maker and city of manufacture were stamped on some silver (see plate 5), but the practice was not

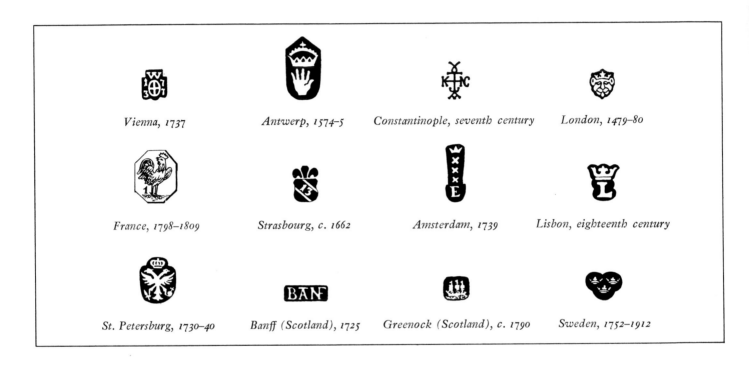

Vienna, 1737   Antwerp, 1574-5   Constantinople, seventh century   London, 1479-80

France, 1798-1809   Strasbourg, c. 1662   Amsterdam, 1739   Lisbon, eighteenth century

St. Petersburg, 1730-40   Banff (Scotland), 1725   Greenock (Scotland), c. 1790   Sweden, 1752-1912

widespread. The term "hallmark" is of English origin, and means the mark of Goldsmiths' Hall—the headquarters in London of the guild of goldsmiths and silversmiths (the Worshipful Company of Goldsmiths), where guild members brought their work to be assayed for purity. Marking was originally introduced as a way for the state to control the use of silver and gold by goldsmiths, who, after all, had access to a commodity of supreme importance—the raw materials of the currency. Statutes requiring hallmarks were introduced and remained most stringent in France and England, and appeared later less stringently in the German states, which were able to produce adequate quantities of the two precious metals by mining in their own territories.

Hallmarking began in France in 1275. The earliest English mark, the leopard's head, dates from 1300. By the seventeenth century hallmarking had been adopted by most European countries. By the second half of the nineteenth century it had become greatly simplified and in some countries could be dropped entirely. The production of gold and silver had reached monumental proportions, and the wealth standard was expressed in terms of gold rather than silver. Silver was even permitted to "disappear" by being consumed in photography, in chemical and industrial processes such as the production of electricity, and by being used as plating on a variety of base metals—a practice that had been illegal in earlier times.

Hallmarks are struck with small steel punches bearing significant devices. In addition to the quality mark, most English and European silver bears marks indicating the maker, the city and the date of manufacture and sometimes whether or not a tax was levied or paid on the piece. Ideally, a complete set of marks can tell the collector where, when and by whom the object was made, although frequently it is possible to determine only one or two of these details because some of the marks are missing, indecipherable or unrecorded.

Our ability to decode marks rests on the huge compilations made in the early twentieth century by Sir Charles Jackson and Marc Rosenberg. Both studied the many statutes governing hallmarks in England and the European countries and correlated them with vast collections of actual marks—arranging them by country, city and maker, and co-ordinating them with marks signifying dates. Their work has been added to and refined by many others who have focused on single countries, and this labor continues. Some of the best marks books have useful indexes in which marks are shown grouped under generic headings: suns, moons, lions, crowns, horses, human figures, plants and so on (these symbols were often derived from the name of the silversmith's shop or were puns on the maker's name). In other books it is necessary to know at least in which country the piece was made before beginning to search for the specific mark.

The stringent regulations enforced on the English and European gold- and silversmiths were not applied in the colonies of North America. Most of the early silversmiths employed their own identifying marks, consisting either of their initials or full name, but there was no additional mark to denote the place of manufacture or the location of the workshop. Up to the third decade of the nineteenth century silversmiths acquired their metal partly from melted-down coinage from various sources, and their metal was consequently of varying alloy. With the growth of a significant silver-producing industry in America in the middle of the nineteenth century, the sterling standard was gradually adopted. The word itself is used on American silver to indicate wares in this standard, and although American silversmiths never were and are not now required to work in the sterling standard, it is against the law to stamp the word "sterling" on any ware that is not in fact of that purity.

Caring for Silver It is axiomatic that sizable collections of silver should be either included in household insurance polices against theft and damage or insured separately. Since silver is easily scratched and dented by careless handling during the course of normal household use, it should always be hand-washed and dried immediately after use; never put it into a dishwasher. Dents, loose handles and feet or similar damage should be entrusted for repair to reputable working silver-smiths.

When silver is not in use or kept in a display cabinet it should be wrapped in tarnish-resistant paper, which can be purchased from certain dealers. Normally, flat ware and stackable pieces like dishes are stored with pads between them to prevent scratching. Because of the chemicals in plastic, it should never be used for storing silver unless a layer of thick cloth or tissue paper is interposed. A periodic cleaning—more frequent in cities with polluted air than in the country—will be necessary to remove tarnish. For this, silver polish, rather than the quicker dips, should be used, although often all that is necessary to remove superficial tarnish is to wash the piece in a very mild solution of warm water and ammonia, thus keeping polishes to a minimum.

Glossary

acanthus, a herbaceous plant whose stylized leaves have been a common ornamental motif in western European decorative arts and architecture.

acid etching, a decorative process in which a corrosive acid is selectively applied to the surface of an object to change the color or the texture of the surface.

ajouré, also called pierced work. Areas of silver in which the background or designs have been entirely cut out of the metal, creating openwork decoration.

alloy, any mixture of metals. In silversmithing, an alloy is a base metal mixed with a precious metal to give the precious metal greater durability; also the the metal combination so obtained.

base metal, any non-precious metal.

bright cut, a sparkling decoration created by cutting shallow elliptical slices into the surface of an object, creating reflective planar surfaces. This decoration has been much used on spoon and fork handles.

Britannia standard, silver of this standard is 95.8 percent pure, with 4.2 percent alloy. The Britannia standard replaced the sterling standard in England in 1697 and remained in mandatory use there until 1720.

burnishing, essentially a polishing process in which the rounded edges and point of a metal blade set in a wooden handle are used to compact and smooth the surface of a formed silver object or to brighten the dull surface of cast silver.

casting, a method of achieving shape for an object by melting the metal and pouring it into a specially prepared mold. On cooling, the silver retains the shape of the mold. Casting can be done in lead or wooden molds or in casting sand.

champlevé enamel, enamel that rests in shallow beds excavated on the surface of an object.

chinoiserie, European interpretation of Oriental design and pictorial motifs. Such decoration became popular in England in the 1680s but was most favored during the rococo period. It was revived in the nineteenth century during the third, fourth and fifth decades.

cut-card work, decorative motifs cut from a sheet of silver and soldered onto the object. Sometimes the motifs themselves are decorated with repoussé or engraving before being cut out and affixed to the host vessel.

electroplating, electrical deposition of gold or silver on the surface of a metal (usually a base metal). In silver production this is usually copper or a white metal.

embossing, similar to repoussé in appearance, but used mainly to create relief designs achieved in one action, such as those impressed by a shaped metal die.

engraving, the decorative use of a line cut from the surface of a finished piece, for pictorial and purely abstract decoration as well as for inscriptions, armorials and crests. Engraving on silver is the equivalent of drawing, since the

effect is gained by the shadow within the cut.

filigree, fine silver, gold or silver-gilt wires twisted and built up in curvilinear designs kept in place with solder applied at points of contact.

flat chasing, an indented linear pattern created on the surface of a finished piece with a fine blunt tool hammered along the path of a design. Broader and usually somewhat deeper than engraving, the technique is often used to outline areas of relief work.

fluting, a surface decoration composed of a series of parallel, usually vertical, concave channels. Derived from classical architecture, fluting was used to ornament the shafts of columns and pilasters.

gadrooning, a surface decoration composed of a series of parallel smooth, rounded ridges juxtaposed vertically, or sometimes set diagonally or in a swirling pattern. In appearance, gadrooning is the opposite of fluting.

hallmarks, marks struck into a silver object at a hall by officers of the guild entrusted with the testing of the purity of the metal used. Different hallmarks denote the quality, date, place of marking, payment of taxes, etc.

martelé, the French term for "hammered," used to describe the decorative effect of the honeycomb-patterned facets left on an object by the planishing hammer. This surface was favored in the second half of the nineteenth and early part of the twentieth centuries by silversmiths who wanted to emphasize the impression of handwork.

matting, a decorative effect created by impressing the surface of the silver article with the point of a tool cut with one of a variety of hatched designs or a series of fine dots. The technique is used to break up the shiny surface of an object by providing contrasting matted areas.

niello, a mixture of sulphur, lead, silver and copper; also the process of decorating metal by filling incised designs with this rich black metallic alloy.

parcel-gilt, the traditional but somewhat obsolete term used to describe objects that are partly gilded.

planishing, the use of a hammer with a smooth, slightly convex head to remove the marks left on an object by the raising process. This is a finishing, not a shaping, technique.

pricking, tiny dots struck in the surface of a vessel to give detail to an engraved pattern or to render dates, initials and occasionally coats of arms and longer inscriptions.

raising, a method for forming hollow vessels by hammering a disc of silver against cast-iron stakes of various sizes and shapes until the vessel achieves the desired form.

repoussé, a method of making patterns or pictures in relief by pushing out ("re-pushing") the surface of the metal from behind.

sinking, a method for forming shallow hollow wares such as bowls or saucers by hammering a disc of silver into a hemispherical recess in a tree trunk or block of wood.

spinning, a mechanical method for forming silver hollow wares in which a flat sheet of silver is pressed against a rapidly rotating wooden chuck.

stamping, a labor-saving process in which silver objects are formed by forcing the metal into a die with a stamping press.

sterling, a silver-copper alloy of 92.5 percent silver and 7.5 percent copper alloy. Sterling was originally the standard for silver coinage in Great Britain. It is now used mainly in Britain, in Scandinavia and the United States as the standard quality for silver goods.

strapwork, a decoration composed mainly of interlaced chased or engraved bands or straps.

swaging, a method for forming metal objects by hand-hammering the metal into a die, or "swage," of the desired form; a slower process than the mechanical stamping process.

wriggle work, linear designs carried out with a roulette, or wheel with a finely crimped edge.

Reading and Reference

General

Brunner, Herbert. *Old Table Silver: A Handbook for Collectors and Amateurs.* Translated by Janet Seligman. New York: Taplinger, 1967.

Hernmarck, Carl. *The Art of the European Silversmith, 1430–1830.* 2 vols. London: Sotheby Parke Bernet, 1977.

Jones, Edward Alfred. *Old Silver of Europe and North America from Early Times to the Nineteenth Century.* Philadelphia: J. B. Lippincott Co., 1928.

Taylor, Gerald. *Art in Silver and Gold.* New York: Dutton, 1964.

Ancient Silver

Forbes, Robert James. *Studies in Ancient Technology,* vols. 7 and 8, *Metallurgy in Antiquity.* 2d ed., rev. New York: William S. Heinman, 1971.

Kent, J. P. C., and K. S. Painter, eds. *Wealth of the Roman World, A.D. 300–700.* London: British Museum Publications, 1977. Exhibition catalogue.

Oliver, Andrew, Jr. *Silver for the Gods: Eight Hundred Years of Greek and Roman Silver.* Toledo, Ohio: Toledo Museum of Art, 1977. Exhibition catalogue.

Strong, Donald Emrys. *Greek and Roman Gold and Silver Plate.* Ithaca, N.Y.: Cornell University Press, 1966.

American Silver

Avery, C. Louise. *Early American Silver.* 1930. Reprint, New York: Russell and Russell, 1968.

Buhler, Kathryn C. *American Silver.* Cleveland and New York: World Publishing Co., 1950.

Carpenter, Charles H., Jr., and Mary Grace Carpenter. *Tiffany Silver.* New York: Dodd, Mead and Co., 1978.

English Silver

Jackson, Charles James. *An Illustrated History of English Plate, Ecclesiastical and Secular.* 2 vols. 1911. Reprint, New York: Dover Publications, 1969.

Hughes, G. Bernard, and Therle Hughes. *Three Centuries of English Domestic Silver, 1500–1820.* New York: Frederick A. Praeger, 1968.

Other

Bøsen, G., and C. A. Bøje. *Old Danish Silver.* Translated by R. Kay. Copenhagen: Hassing, 1949.

Churchill, S. J. A. *The Goldsmiths of Italy.* Edited by C. G. E. Bunt. London: M. Hopkinson and Co., Ltd., 1926.

Dennis, Faith. *Three Centuries of French Domestic Silver: Its Makers and Its Marks.* New York: Metropolitan Museum of Art, 1960.

Finlay, Ian. *Scottish Gold and Silver Work.* London: Chatto & Windus, 1956.

Gans, M. H., and T. M. Duyvené de Wit-Klinkhamer. *Dutch Silver.* Translated by O. van Oss. London: Faber and Faber, 1961.

Johnson, Ada, and Marshall Johnson. *Hispanic Silverwork.* New York: Hispanic Society of America, 1944.

Hallmarks

Beuque, Émile. *Dictionnaire des poinçons officiels français & étrangers, anciens & modernes.* 2 vols. Paris: F. de Nobele, 1925–8.

Bulgari, C. G. *Argentieri, gemmari e orafi d'Italia.* 2 vols. Rome: Lorenzo Del Turco, 1958–1969.

Currier, Ernest M. *Marks of Early American Silversmiths.* Edited by Kathryn C. Buhler. Portland, Maine: The Southworth-Anthoenson Press, 1938.

Ensko, Stephen Guernsey. *American Silversmiths and Their Marks.* 3 vols. New York: Robert Ensko, 1927–1948.

Grimwade, Arthur. *London Goldsmiths, 1697–1837.* London: Faber and Faber, 1976.

Jackson, Charles James. *English Goldsmiths and Their Marks.* 2d ed. 1921. Reprint, New York: Dover Publications, 1964.

Rainwater, Dorothy T. *Encyclopedia of American Silver Manufacturers.* New York: Crown Publishers, 1975.

Rosenberg, Marc. *Der Goldschmiede Merkzeichen.* 4 vols. 3d ed. 1890. Reprint, Frankfurt am Main: Frankfurter Verlags-Anstalt, A.G., 1922–8.

Some Public Collections of Silver

UNITED STATES

Baltimore:	The Baltimore Museum of Art
	The Walters Art Gallery
Boston:	Museum of Fine Arts
Chicago:	The Art Institute of Chicago
Cincinnati:	Cincinnati Art Museum
Cleveland:	Cleveland Museum of Art
Detroit:	The Detroit Institute of Arts
Houston:	The Houston Museum of Fine Arts
Los Angeles:	Los Angeles County Museum of Art
Minneapolis:	The Minneapolis Institute of Arts
New Haven, Conn.:	Yale University Art Gallery
New York City:	The Brooklyn Museum
	Cooper-Hewitt Museum,
	the Smithsonian Institution's National Museum of Design
	The Metropolitan Museum of Art
	The New-York Historical Society
Philadelphia:	Philadelphia Museum of Art
San Francisco:	The Fine Arts Museum of San Francisco
	M. H. de Young Memorial Museum
St. Louis:	The St. Louis Art Museum
Toledo, Ohio:	The Toledo Museum of Art
Washington, D.C.:	Smithsonian Institution
	National Museum of American History
	(formerly National Museum of History and Technology)
Williamsburg, Va.:	Colonial Williamsburg
Williamstown, Mass.:	Sterling and Francine Clark Art Institute
Winterthur, Del.:	The Henry Francis du Pont Winterthur Museum

OTHER

Amsterdam:	Rijksmuseum
Berlin:	Kunstgewerbemuseum
Copenhagen:	Det Danske Kunstindustrimuseum
Dresden:	Staatliche Kunstsammlungen
Dublin:	National Museum of Ireland
Edinburgh:	Royal Scottish Museum
Leningrad:	State-Hermitage Museum
Lisbon:	Museu Nacional de Arte Antigua
London:	British Museum Victoria and Albert Museum
Montreal:	Montreal Museum of Fine Arts
Moscow:	Kremlin Museums: State Armory Museum
Munich:	Bayerisches Nationalmuseum
Ottawa:	National Gallery of Canada
Paris:	Musée du Louvre Musée des Arts Décoratifs
Stockholm:	Nationalmuseum
Vienna:	Kunsthistorisches Museum
Warsaw:	Muzeum Narodowe w Warszawie
Zurich:	Kunstgewerbemuseum

Index

Acknowledgments

Cooper-Hewitt staff members have been responsible for the following contributions to the series: concept, Lisa Taylor; administration, John Dobkin, Christian Rohlfing, David McFadden and Kurt Struver; coordination, Peter Scherer and Pamela Theodoredis. In addition, valuable help has been provided by S. Dillon Ripley, Joseph Bonsignore, Susan Hamilton and Robert W. Mason of the Smithsonian Institution, as well as by the late Warren Lynch, Gloria Norris and Edward E. Fitzgerald of Book-of-the-Month Club, Inc.

AUTHOR'S ACKNOWLEDGMENTS I wish to thank my colleagues at the Metropolitan Museum of Art and at sister institutions here and abroad for their helpfulness, expressed in so many ways, during the course of writing this book—especially that of David McFadden of the Cooper-Hewitt Museum, who read the manuscript, and of Margaret Hillery and Pamela Gibney. I congratulate Lisa Taylor on the concept for the series, and also thank her for providing the most dulcet of editors in Brenda Gilchrist and Nancy Akre. I am grateful, too, to Ann Adelman, Neal Jones and Lisa Little for assistance along the way. Finally, I thank Elizabeth, Ian and Crispin for uncomplainingly bearing my many absences from them.

JESSIE McNAB

Credits

Zuppiera

Vaso p Bottiglia e Porta bic
sotto da dismettersi

Piatto

Salziera

Portaaglio

Sgom

Tazza p il